THE
FARMER'S MARKET
COOKBOOK

RICHARD RUBEN

The Lyons Press
Guilford, Connecticut
An imprint of The Globe Pequot Press

Offered to My Parents

❧ CONTENTS ❧

With a wish I acknowledge
Lives vital for my being
Grateful that you shared

Leza Lowitz, Shogo Oketani, Suzen O'Rouke, Hope Flamm, Edith Merrit, Andy Pound of Greenleaf Produce, Charles and Kim Wasser, Dennis Sneyers, Dubravka Bondulic, Carole Ferrara, Tim Healea, Shelly Leinheardt, Kaleh Friedman, Vince Deuschel, Tom Fox, Marie Romano, Shaun Bridgman, Christopher Kodama, Mary Bartolini, Mark Kornspan, Gregory Stanford, Sheila Kash, the Machowskys, Karyn and Tabytha Ruben, all my students, and my editor, Becky Koh.

❦ INTRODUCTION ❦

There is no longer a sense of seasonal foods in this world. Meats come to grocers shrink-wrapped, vegetables arrive frozen from multinational manufacturers, and fruits are flown in from far-off countries. This disenfranchises us from nature's cycle and timing. As a chef, I am totally dependent on the earth and the cornucopia it offers; I have found that cooking is always simpler and more visually vibrant when I choose foods at the peak of their season and flavor.

Cooking seasonally means developing a keen eye and sensitive nose as you traverse the aisles of nature's store. The trimmings of each season are color-coded—spring's plate is drenched with verdant green leaves, tender stalks, and gentle herbs; summer is resplendent with myriad reds, oranges, and yellows creating texture and bold, redolent assaults; autumn's quieting is rich with umber root vegetables and a second hurrah of green leaves. This rainbow presentation is an initial starting point for setting a menu.

I discovered the excitement of the green market while living in Australia. Through my weekly jaunts to Sydney's Paddy's Market, I connected with nature's rhythm and reveled in the great unknown with each culinary discovery the seasons offered. One spring day—no, it was autumn (I never did get used to the reverse of the seasons Down Under)—I went to the market yearning for something new and ripe. I roamed the aisles in hopes of being seduced by something that would placate my out-of-season timing. There, in a quiet corner away from the hustle and bustle, squeezed between crates of oranges and shiny green peppers, stood a farmer with fresh knobs of turmeric, bundles of cilantro, rows of chilies, and fussy okra adorning his table. His labor bore beautiful, healthy produce, but it was an odd, inhospitable-looking thing that intrigued me. It was the size of a softball, had a mottled, reptilian skin, and was very dense to the touch. I had found it—something new, something that piqued my creative craving.

Excitedly, I inquired about this odd-looking thing, which I was told by the farmer was called *breadfruit*. I felt slightly deflated, since I was really seeking a savory flavor and thought I'd have to be content with an exotic fruit salad that day. But the farmer explained that the breadfruit's starchy interior could be baked, steamed, or stewed. The flame of my desire got turned up again. Questioning him further, I asked for his favorite recipe. This brought our conversation to a halt. He was not the cook in his home, but he turned to his wife and repeated my question. She and I had a long and informative exchange concerning the breadfruit, as well as the usage of chilies, toasting of curries, and how to make a coconut chutney. I was agog with ideas for the breadfruit, so I bought one and carried it away in my sack. Once home I made a sublime breadfruit curry stew with toasted cashews and coconut that became the most requested stew of that summer—I mean, winter.

The green market not only thrills my senses, it connects me to the community in which I live. There seems to be a phenomenon at the market where smiles overtake stern glares and people greet each other with kindly hellos. To become a regular at a market is to hold a membership in a fraternity—an ancient association where knowledge and experience are exchanged as nourishment changes hands.

The Farmer's Market Cookbook pays homage to nature and the palate that it offers for our cooking and sharing pleasure. Divided into three parts—Spring, Summer, and Autumn—the book will guide you through the ripening seasons and the many food options available to you. The recipes are meant as a road map, which allows you to navigate your own local markets—be it a green market, grocer's produce aisle, or your own backyard garden—and give you a sense of comfort when making a choice. The winter season in the majority of this country is a time when the earth rests and is blanketed by a frosty covering. The foods available to us during this time of repose have ripened during autumn. In my view, options are the key to cooking. You must feel empowered to make substitutions according to what is available to you. Each part ends with a series of blank pages that should be used as your culinary journal. Take notes on the foods that were available at a particular moment in the season, dishes made, or ideas to be explored further the next time the season is upon you.

These note pages will become a vital source of information regarding favorite varieties of apples or a newly discovered variety of potato. I go to the markets yearly, and inevitably a new heirloom variety has been re-introduced or a farmer is trying a new crop, and now my choices have more than doubled. Of course, I believe in trying everything new at least once.

Charts peppered throughout the book will help you to learn the seasonal availability of foods and the possible ways to use them. These are in no way definitive lists; your local area is going to offer a profusion of items to add to them. There are also items listed that only grow in certain regions of our wonderfully diverse country. Living in the northeast, I anxiously await the arrival of northern California's artichokes in early spring. To completely satisfy my various cravings, I must, at times, look beyond the immediate land that surrounds me. For those who live in regions where hard chill never puts the earth to sleep, you'll find the bounty of spring and summer lasts longer and blurs into each other. Conversely, autumn's offerings may be somewhat truncated.

Without question, the best way to learn about the seasonal availability of food is to walk through the market, speak to growers, take notes, and most important: *Be in the moment in the market!*

SPRING

The market fills up . . .
Ramps . . . Fiddleheads . . . Pansies . . . Herbs . . .
and so do I

❦ SPRING'S BOUNTY ❦

The region of the country where you live and the severity of the winter past will determine when spring will start pushing forth its tight, tender buds. I start watching the local markets in late March, and by late April I am reaping the rewards of the season of renewal.

Vegetables	Herbs	Fruits
Artichokes	Chervil	Mango
Arugula	Chives	Rhubarb
Asparagus	Cilantro	Strawberries
Broccoli rabe	Loveage	
Carrots	Mint	
Chicory	Parsley	
Fava bean	Thyme	
Fennel		
Fiddlehead ferns		
Green onions		
Garlic sprouts		
Leeks		
Lettuce greens		
Mushrooms		
Peas sprouts		
Radishes		
Ramps (wild leeks)		
Sorrel		
Snow peas		
Spinach		
Swiss chard		
Watercress		

A quick definition: an herb is the leafy part of the plant. The stem, root, seeds, or bark is defined as the spice.

The Wednesday market in Santa Monica, California, probably taught me the most about herbs, given the profusion available there, and it sent me into culinary and olfactory overdrive. Fortunately, there are now many fresh herbs available year-round throughout the country, and we are no longer restricted to commercially dried herbs. Yes, fresh herbs tend to be sandy and will need to be washed, though this is no reason not to use them. It is also important to dry them well before chopping, which prevents them from blackening. I place mine in a salad spinner as a quick drying technique. I prefer to chop my herbs roughly; chopping herbs finely releases too much flavor onto the cutting board and into the kitchen, leaving very little left for the dish—and I love experiencing the full explosion of fresh herbs in my mouth.

I've found very few fresh herbs that freeze well. Most of them blacken and break down with the chill. There are, however, herbs such as bay laurel, verbena, and Kaffir lime leaves that do tend to survive freezing—since they usually have thicker, tougher leaves. To freeze these herbs, make sure they are completely dry and then place them in an air-tight bag or plastic container. To preserve the fragrance of other herbs, I puree them with either canola or almond oil to create a pesto-like paste. The pastes will survive 6 months in the freezer. When ready for use, allow the pastes to sit at room temperature for about 10 minutes so they can be easily scooped. Always remember to label the jars, since one green paste looks very much like another! I then use the various pastes in marinades, sautés, soups, and rubs for roasts.

You can dry your own herbs simply by tying loosely bound bunches to a rafter in the attic. If you live in an apartment, you can tie bunches to a hanger and place them in a closet for 1 week. Any cool, dark place will do. After you dry the herbs, place them in a sealed opaque container. Then, ideally, store them in the freezer, since light and warmth destroy the flavor of a dried herb. The cold, dark environment of the freezer helps maintain their flavor best. Most dried herbs have about a 3- to 4-month shelf life. A dried herb's flavor is slightly strong due to the evaporation of the water content, as the essence that creates its fragrance also becomes more pronounced.

Finally, if you've bought flowering herbs, they are edible. Any plant that offers an edible leaf also gives you its bloom to enjoy. Be aware though, that once an herb has started to flower, the energy the plant gives toward seed production causes the flavor in the leaf to fade.

TYPES OF HERBS

Basil   This is probably the king of herbs, known for its versatility and universal appeal. Basil's flavor fades quickly once cut, so it's important to use it as soon as possible. Store the cut basil stem in water, as you would fresh flowers, making sure no leaves are submerged in the water. You will get about a 3-day shelf life, depending on how fresh the basil was when it was purchased. This herb's flavor also fades fast when cooked, so I always add it toward the end of the cooking process. Basil is one of the friendliest of herbs and marries well to most other herbs. Try the many different varieties on the market such as Thai, cinnamon, lemon, fino (a personal favorite), or opal.

Bay laurel   This is commonly referred to as the bay leaf, that ubiquitous soup perfumer. The flavor difference between fresh and dried is unbelievable; and once you've used the fresh, it will be difficult to go back to the dried. Fortunately, the bay laurel is a leaf that freezes well. I take it right from the freezer to the pot.

Borage   The leaves and flowers of this herb have culinary usages. The leaves are best used tossed into salads, and have a wonderful cucumber-like taste. The light purple flowers are a wonder in iced teas and as garnishes for salad greens and pastries.

✠ **Chamomile** This is a bushy green leaf plant with multiple yellow and white flowers and is best used steeped as a tea, either hot or iced. Alternatively, fill your bathtub and add these gentle redolent sprigs and take a wonderfully relaxing bath.

✠ **Chervil** One of the herbs of spring, it has a very faint anise fragrance, which fades easily, and has delicate, small fernlike leaves. It is one of the herbs that makes up *fines herbes* along with parsley, chive, and tarragon. As a garnish leaf, it is superior given its light, feathery look. It is one of two herbs whose stem has culinary uses . . . cilantro being the other.

✠ **Chives** The most mild of the onion family, this grasslike herb has great versatility and pairs well with almost any other herb. Store in a container filled with water, cut—end down—in the refrigerator. Or, better yet, grow your own—it does quite well in a window box and flourishes all summer long. The purplish flowers are edible and are delicious in salads or as a flavoring agent for a vinegar. Chinese chives have flattened blades and are a bit more pungent. They make a perfect substitution anytime you find them. Another popular variety is garlic chive.

✠ **Cilantro** Also known as coriander or Chinese parsley, this herb is inextricably associated with Mexican cooking, but is actually native to southern Europe. It is a plant that allows 100-percent usage. The stem of this plant is not very fibrous, and I use it right along with the leaves. The roots, once washed well, are also edible, chopped into stews, soups, and marinades. Placed in water, especially if the roots are attached, this herb will survive for 1 week in the refrigerator. If you are one of the many who find this herb "soapy," try pairing it with some mint or basil to help balance its experience.

✠ **Dill** Used extensively throughout European cooking, this feathery leaf herb is found year-round. It wilts quickly, so expect a 3- to 4-day shelf life. Dried dill loses it flavor dramatically. It's a natural with fish and chicken or snipped into a potato salad. Make a dill vinegar using 1 part white wine vinegar and ¼ part lemon juice.

✳ **Hyssop**   A member of the mint family, with strongly scented leaves that are slightly bitter, it makes a lovely iced tea. It is also used to fragrance poaching liquids for fish, or toss the torn leaves into a green salad.

✳ **Kaffir lime**   A tough, aromatic leaf that originated in eastern India, it can be found fresh, dried, and frozen. It has a pungent, lemony aroma and is often used in Asian cuisine. Make a paste with lemon grass, chilies, shallots, and garlic to use as a marinade or curry base.

✳ **Lavender**   This beautiful, aromatic flower is used sparingly for its fragrance. Too much can overpower and give a "soapy" taste. Choose lavender with buds that have not quite opened, since their flavor is best. A suspicion of lavender goes into the mixture *Herbes de Provence*. When making a ratatouille, add a pinch of lavender into this Provençal classic.

✳ **Lemon balm**   A heart-shaped leaf with a subtle lemon scent, it works wonderfully in teas, with fish, or tossed in a vegetable or fruit salad. Store in the refrigerator for about 3 days wrapped in some paper towel to keep it dry.

✳ **Lemon grass**   These long stalks (approximately 12 to 14 inches) have gained fame through the popularity of Southeast Asian cooking. They can be found year-round in most Asian markets as well as better green markets, but are best used during the heat of the summer months. They can be frozen wrapped in plastic wrap and then aluminum foil for up to 3 months. They are not pleasant to eat due to their very fibrous nature; however, their aromatic offering is exquisite. Make a sun tea with sliced ginger root and lemon grass, or a paste with cilantro, mint, basil, green onion, and chili to use in coconut stews or as a rub for meats and fish.

✳ **Loveage**   This is an assertive celery-flavored herb that you'll find in the warming months of spring. Its hollow stem drinks up water easily; refrigerated in a container with some water, it will give you about 5 days worth of green leaves. You might want to change the water every few days. Its flavor holds up well in stew and soups and marries well to the base aromatic collection of parsley, thyme, bay leaves, and chives.

- **Marjoram** This herb can easily be replaced with oregano, though marjoram has a slightly less potent flavor. When dried, this herb retains its flavor quite well, and in Sicilian and Mexican dishes, the dried variety is preferred. Its potency comes through, so judicious additions are recommended. Classically, it's paired with basil and parsley in tomato sauce, or you can try it with rosemary, mint, garlic, and lemon for a strong marinade for meats and chicken. Refrigerate in a water-filled container for about 5 days.

- **Mint** This cousin to basil represents a huge family of herbal possibilities: apple mint, black mint, Corsican mint, chocolate mint, peppermint, spearmint . . . try them all! When you get to the market and are assailed with a slew of choices, you must scratch and sniff each one, since they each have a slightly different aroma. Mint is recognized as the "dessert" herb, but try to break it out of its box by pairing it with cilantro, basil, or rosemary. Refrigerate in a water-filled container for about 1 week.

- **Nasturtium** Known for its flower that garnishes plates and salads, its young, tender leaves add a lovely, peppery flavor to salads as well. Make a compound butter with the flowers for an elegant service—just soften unsalted butter, mix in gingerly torn petals, and then refrigerate. The compound butter will last approximately 3 weeks.

- **Parsley** Flat-leaf, otherwise known as Italian, and the much-maligned curly variety are the two players in this field. I prefer the Italian variety, since I find it more robust in flavor and like its texture better. However, they are interchangeable in any recipe. This is perhaps the most ubiquitous of herbs found in one of the two varieties throughout the country year-round. Refrigerate in a jar filled with some water for about 1 week.

- **Rosemary** The friend of potatoes, chicken, and grilled meats, this herb is readily found year-round, except in the colder areas of the country. The long stems, if they are woody enough, act as wonderful skewers for chicken, vegetable, or lamb kebobs. Strip away about two-thirds of the leaves before skewering. This is an herb that tends to overpower the other herbs it is paired with. Use with parsley, oregano, basil, thyme, and chives, but use twice the amount of the other herbs to allow a more complex flavor to come through. Store in the refrigerator for a week to 10 days.

- **Sage** One of the last herbs of autumn, it has a strong aroma, but marries well to a base of parsley, thyme, and chives. It's perfect for poultry, but try it torn into pasta with cherry tomatoes and olive oil. Store in the refrigerator wrapped in a paper towel for up to 1 week. For an incredible treat, seek out pineapple sage, which has an aroma that is without compare. This sage makes a wonderful tea and is great with salmon, swordfish, and chicken.

- **Savory** There are two varieties of this herb: summer and winter. The winter variety is slightly less aromatic and has tougher leaves. It has a fragrance that smells like a combination of thyme, parsley, and marjoram—and welcomes vegetables, meats, and fish. It has needlelike leaves that are attached to short, stubby stems. This herb lasts a good week kept in a water-filled container in the refrigerator or can be dried successfully. This is a "party herb" in so far as it pairs well with most other herbs. Try it with sage in your turkey stuffing.

- **Sorrel** Herb or green leaf vegetable? Well, it depends on how you are using it. It has a fantastic lemony taste with a slightly grassy quality that unfortunately fades quickly when cooked. The leaf looks like small, smooth spinach leaf—only a lighter shade of green. Use this puckering green leaf in salads, pestos, and salsas. It is found from spring through autumn, though as the season moves along, the leaf become slightly tougher and, if allowed to flower, loses some of it potency.

- **Tarragon** This is a licorice in the form of thin, tapered green leaves—an essential of French flavor. This strong flavor, when used in a smaller portion, marries well with other herbs such as Italian parsley, thyme, chives, and chervil. It is one of the herbs in *fines herbes* along with parsley, chives, and chervil. It naturally enhances fish and chicken and makes a tasty vinegar. Refreigerate in a water-filled container for up to 1 week.

✠ **Texas tarragon**   Also known as Mexican mint. I discovered it on the East Coast a few years ago. It has a strong tarragon/mint flavor, which should be used judiciously. It becomes available in midsummer and lasts through the waning season. Use it along with onion, garlic, and thyme when making Green Rice (page 97). Refrigerate in a water-filled container for about 5 days.

✠ **Thyme**   A cornerstone herb in the culinary pantry, this is one of the most versatile and friendly of herbs. It marries happily to other aromatics or shines through on its own. Store wrapped in paper towel in the refrigerator for 1 week or longer. Look for other varieties such as pepper thyme, lemon thyme, and caraway thyme.

✠ **Verbena**   This Mexican native sends me over the top. In cooler climates the plant gets to be about two feet high, but in the warmer areas it erupts into a bushy three-foot-high plant. Highly fragrant with one of the best lemony scents in the herbal world, it can flavor fish, vegetables, chicken, desserts, and teas. The leaves are tough but can be finely minced or pureed and then added to a dish. When used whole, the leaves are discarded, not unlike the bay leaf. This leaf freezes very well—leave on the stem and place in a plastic bag for up to 3 months of heavenly enjoyment.

STARTERS

SAUTÉED FIDDLEHEAD FERNS

YIELDS 8 SERVINGS

I so clearly remember the first time I came across this strange, primitive-looking vegetable. I was a culinary student in San Francisco, and I thought I had just discovered one of the seven wonders of the cooking world. I became an immediate fan of these fleeting morsels and share them with clients, students, friends, and family every spring.

1½ pounds fiddlehead ferns

3 tablespoons toasted sesame oil

½ cup soy sauce

1 tablespoon sesame seeds

Black pepper to taste

Wash the fiddlehead ferns very well. Place them in a large bowl filled with cold water. Gently rub the ferns under the water to dislodge any browned leaves and debris. Then skim the top of the water to remove the leaves that float to the top and rinse the ferns well under cold running water. Slightly drain the cleaned ferns in a colander and set aside.

Heat a 10-inch sauté pan to hot, then add the sesame oil and the fiddlehead ferns. The ferns should still have some water clinging to them and will spit and spatter when placed in the oil. However, this water is important since it helps to cook the fiddleheads. Sauté the fiddleheads for about 5 minutes, tossing them often. Pour in the soy sauce and continue to cook for about 3 more minutes. Toss with the sesame seeds and black pepper to taste and serve immediately.

Notes

Fiddlehead ferns are the young, tender, coiled fronds of the ostrich fern and are, for me, the one sure harbinger of spring. By late March I am eagerly awaiting their arrival in the market and continually badger my favorite growers as to when I can expect them. Be sure to buy tightly wound ferns; once they unfurl, they acquire an unpleasant flavor. Fiddlehead ferns have a short window of opportunity—approximately 4 weeks—but they are a food that makes me feel like I am grazing from the primordial forest. They are delicious deep fried, coated in a light batter, added to an omelet, or simply blanched and tossed into a salad. They have a nutty taste with a slightly lettucelike character.

FIDDLEHEAD FERN RISOTTO

YIELDS 8 TO 10 SERVINGS

The preparation of risotto is truly a labor of love, like the care a doting mother gives to her newborn child. Yet, every season I am lured back to the stove, heavy wooden spoon in hand, to stir this rice-based concoction that, regardless of the flavor treatment, fills my stomach and heart with joy.

> 1 pound fiddlehead ferns—washed well
>
> 6 cups chicken or vegetable stock
>
> ½ cup olive oil
>
> 1 medium onion—finely diced
>
> 2 shallots—finely diced
>
> 2 cups Aborio rice
>
> 2 tablespoons thyme leaves—roughly chopped
>
> ½ cup white wine
>
> Salt and black pepper to taste
>
> 1 cup Parmesan cheese—grated

Bring a four-quart pot of water to a boil and blanch the fiddlehead ferns for 3 minutes. Strain and refresh under cold water to stop the cooking process. Set aside.

Bring the 6 cups of stock to a boil in a 2-quart saucepan.

Meanwhile, heat a thick bottomed, four-quart saucepan over a medium flame and add the olive oil. Add the onion and shallots and cook over a low heat until soft and translucent, about 3 to 5 minutes. Add the rice and cook for a few minutes to coat the rice well with the oil. Start adding the hot stock, a ladleful at a time, stirring the rice mixture constantly. Keep stirring until the liquid has been absorbed, then add another ladleful. When you've added about half of the stock, mix in the thyme and then continue adding more stock. Continue in this manner until all the stock is incorporated, approximately 30 minutes. Just prior to adding the last ladleful, stir in the wine and fiddlehead ferns. Season with salt and pepper to taste. Add the Parmesan cheese and serve.

ORECCHIETTE PASTA WITH
FIDDLEHEAD FERN

The orecchiette pasta is one of my favorite shapes. Its name means "little ears" in Italian, and its small disk shape complements the fiddleheads perfectly. Plus, what could be better than three of my favorite foods together in a single dish: the orecchiette, fiddleheads, and olives? Of course, any one of your favorite pastas will work here, such as fussili, orzo, or tortellini. The preparation is always quick and easy.

1 cup orecchiette pasta—uncooked

1 pint fiddlehead ferns (approx. ¼ pound)—washed well, drained, and all brown leaves discarded

20 Kalamata olives—pitted and cut in half

1 bunch watercress—roughly chopped

2 garlic cloves—crushed to a paste

¼ cup extra virgin olive oil

⅛ cup white wine vinegar

⅛ teaspoon cayenne pepper

Salt and black pepper to taste

Bring a 4-quart pot of water to a boil. Depending on whether you are using fresh or dried pasta determines the next step. If using fresh pasta, add the fiddleheads first and cook for about 3 minutes before adding the pasta. Then cook together for another 2 to 3 minutes, or until the pasta is done. If using dried pasta, add the pasta first and cook for about 5 to 6 minutes. Then add the fiddleheads for another 5 minutes of cooking.

Drain in a colander. Promptly, while the pasta and fiddleheads are still warm, toss with the olives, watercress, garlic, olive oil, vinegar, cayenne pepper, salt, and black pepper to thoroughly incorporate. Serve warm.

SWISS CHARD WONTON RAVIOLIS

YIELDS 8 SERVINGS

Notes

You may use any green leaf in this recipe. If you are using a thin, green like spinach, blanch it in boiling water, drain, and squeeze out the excess water. Then proceed to assemble the raviolis.

Wonton skins are such a versatile product. Outside of Asian markets, you can find them in the refrigerated section of the grocery store. If they are difficult to find, you may want to buy a small store of them whenever you get the chance and freeze them. Place the package of wontons in the refrigerator and let them defrost in the course of about 2 hours. The uncooked raviolis themselves freeze very well, though you must freeze them in a single layer before storing them in a plastic bag or container. Otherwise, they'll stick to each other and you'll find yourself serving very large raviolis.

> 1 bunch red or white Swiss chard (approx. 2 pounds)
>
> 2 tablespoons + $\frac{1}{2}$ cup olive oil
>
> 2 garlic cloves—finely minced
>
> $\frac{3}{4}$ cup Parmesan cheese
>
> Salt and black pepper to taste
>
> 1 package wonton wrappers (approximately 50 count)
>
> $\frac{1}{4}$ cup cornstarch

Remove the rib from the leaves of the Swiss chard. Wash both, but keep them separate.

Bring a four-quart pot of water to a boil and cook the leaves for 3 to 4 minutes. Drain. Roughly chop the leaves. Meanwhile, dice the ribs into small pieces and sauté in 2 tablespoons of olive oil with the garlic for 5 minutes. Drain the ribs through a fine sieve over a large bowl collecting the liquid given off from the cooked ribs. Reserve the liquid.

Toss the Swiss chard leaf, rib, and Parmesan cheese together. Taste and correct seasoning with salt and pepper.

Place about a tablespoon's worth of the Swiss chard mixture in the center of a wonton skin. Lightly dampen the edges with water and lay another wonton skin on top. Carefully squeeze out any air from the ravioli and pinch the edges to seal. Place the completed raviolis on a tray lightly dusted with cornstarch (this helps prevent the raviolis from sticking to the surface). Continue with the rest.

Preheat the oven to 350°F.

Lightly oil a baking tray and lay the raviolis down in a single layer. Lightly brush the tops of the raviolis with olive oil. Place in the oven and bake for 10 minutes, or until golden brown.

Bring the reserved Swiss chard liquid to a boil, season with salt and pepper, and add the remaining oil to the liquid. Drizzle over each serving.

LINGUINI WITH CLAM SAUCE

YIELDS 6 SERVINGS

When I was in Sicily I had the original version of this dish, and the clams they used there were the tiniest, most tender bivalves I have ever had. So I try to find the smallest clams I can when replicating it here in the States. Shellfish in general do not sit well keeping warm as they tend to get tough. You can get this entire recipe ready up to the point of cooking the clams well in advance and then add the clams just prior to serving.

1 pound linguini

3 tablespoons extra virgin olive oil

1 tablespoon garlic clove—sliced thinly

½ teaspoons ground black pepper

½ teaspoon red chili flakes

¾ cup dry white wine

48 littleneck clams—scrubbed clean

¼ cup Italian parsley leaves—roughly chopped

2 tablespoons lemon juice

½ cup Parmesan cheese—grated

Bring a six-quart pot of water to a boil.

At the same time, heat a high-sided 10-inch sauté pan over medium heat and add the olive oil. Add the garlic, pepper, and red chili flakes and cook for a minute to release their aromatic flavors. Immediately add the wine and clams and cover with a tight-fitting lid. Cook the clams for 10 to 12 minutes or until the clams have opened.

Add the linguini to the boiling water, cook according to the instructions on the package, and then drain.

Toss the linguini, parsley, and lemon juice immediately into the clam mixture and serve. You want the clams to be waiting for the pasta, but do not let them wait too long or the clams will toughen. Garnish each plate with grated Parmesan cheese.

ASPARAGUS AND SAFFRON RISOTTO

This is a great basic recipe for risotto. You can make it here with asparagus or with sugar snap peas that arrive later in the season. Try sweet, crisp corn kernels in summer or finely diced pumpkin in the fall.

½ teaspoon saffron threads

½ cup white wine

1 pound asparagus

6 cups chicken or vegetable stock

½ cup olive oil

1 medium onion—finely diced

1½ cups Aborio rice

Salt and black pepper to taste

1 cup Parmesan cheese—grated

Crumble the saffron threads into the white wine.

Trim the asparagus ends and discard. Cut the asparagus into ½-inch pieces. Reserve the tips.

Bring 3 cups of water to a boil in a 2-quart saucepan, and blanch the asparagus tips for 1 minute in boiling water. Drain the tips and run under cold water to stop them from cooking further. Reserve them to use as a garnish for the risotto.

Bring the stock to a boil.

Heat a thick-bottomed, four-quart saucepan over medium heat and add the olive oil. Lower the heat, add the onion, and cook until soft and translucent, about 3 to 5 minutes. Add the rice and cook for about 3 minutes to coat the rice well with oil. Start adding the hot stock, a ladleful at a time, stirring the rice mixture constantly. Keep stirring until the liquid has been absorbed, then add another ladleful. Continue in this manner until all of the stock is incorporated, approximately 30 minutes. Just prior to adding the last ladleful, stir in the saffron/wine mixture and asparagus. Correct seasoning with salt and pepper. Add the Parmesan cheese, garnish with the asparagus tips, and serve.

WILD MUSHROOM STRUDEL

YIELDS 6 TO 8 SERVINGS

Notes

This is such a great presentation that once you get over the fear of working with phyllo dough, you will start to think up myriad possibilities for this recipe. Some good substitutions for the wild mushrooms include goat cheese and asparagus; ground lamb, pine nuts, and mint; sun-dried tomatoes, grilled eggplant, grated Parmesan, and fresh herbs. The really wonderful thing about these strudels is that they freeze very well. Place the entire uncooked strudel in the freezer for 15 minutes to let it slightly chill, and then remove it and wrap it well in aluminum foil. It will keep for up 2 months. Do not defrost the strudel, just add an extra 10 to 15 minutes to the baking time.

Whenever I cook with wild mushroom, I am immediately transported back to a market in San Francisco. I was fresh out of culinary school and working as a chef for a catering company. One spring day I headed to the market seeking something special for an upcoming event. It was then I spied a selection of a dozen or more types of mushrooms. Where have they been all my life—shiitakes, matsutakes, pompoms, corral chanterels, oysters, enoki, black trumpets? I grew up in suburbia and the only fungi I knew was the cultivated white button. As I collected the loamy black trumpets, a tiny baby snake slithered out of a mushroom's fold to reveal itself. I honored its dwindling home and allowed it to glide securely into the depths of the pile. As I resumed my gathering, my mind was now conveyed to a moist, shadowy forest.

$1\frac{1}{2}$ **pounds assorted wild mushrooms such as shiitakes, oysters, and hen of the woods**

$\frac{1}{4}$ **cup dried morel mushrooms**

2 tablespoons olive oil

3 shallots—sliced thin

2 garlic cloves—diced

$\frac{1}{4}$ **cup brandy**

$\frac{1}{4}$ **cup pine nuts—lightly toasted, roughly chopped**

$\frac{1}{2}$ **cup Italian parsley—leaves only, chopped**

$\frac{1}{8}$ **cup thyme—leaves only, chopped**

Salt and black pepper to taste

$\frac{1}{4}$ **pound phyllo dough—at room temperature**

$\frac{1}{2}$ **pound unsalted butter—melted**

Clean the fresh wild mushrooms with a damp kitchen towel and roughly chop them.

In a fine mesh colander, rinse the dried morels under running water to rid them of any dirt and grit. Soak the morels in $\frac{1}{2}$ cup of hot water for 30 minutes. Drain and reserve their soaking liquid, then roughly chop the morels.

Heat a 10- or 12-inch sauté pan to hot and add the olive oil. Sauté the shallots until lightly golden, about 5 minutes, and then add the garlic and the fresh wild mushrooms and continue cooking for 5 more minutes. Add the brandy and morels along with reserved liquid. Bring to a boil and then reduce to a simmer. Cook until the liquid has evaporated, about 5 minutes. Mix in the pine nuts and herbs, and season with salt and pepper. Cool the mushroom mixture.

Preheat the oven to 375°F.

Lay out a sheet of phyllo flat, and using a pastry brush, lightly paint the sheet with the melted butter. Always start brushing the phyllo with melted butter from the outer edges working your way inward, since the phyllo starts to dry on the outer fringes first. Place an additional 5 sheets on top of this first one, buttering each layer. Keep the phyllo you are not working with spread out flat under a damp kitchen towel to prevent it from drying out. Once all 6 sheets of phyllo are buttered and layered on top of each other, spread half of the mushroom mixture along the length of the bottom third of the phyllo. Then carefully roll up the phyllo over the mushroom mixture and continue to roll the mixture completely into a tight log. Once you have rolled the strudel halfway, you will have edges that you should fold in, as if you where wrapping a gift, and then continue to roll up the strudel completely. Transfer the roll to a parchment-lined baking tray. Cut 3 to 4 slashes in the top of the strudel. These cuts allow steam to escape and help prevent the strudel from bursting. Lightly brush the strudel with some melted butter. Repeat this with the remaining mushroom mixture to make a second strudel. Place in the oven and bake for 15 minutes or until golden and crisp. Slice the strudel on an angle while warm and serve.

FAVA BEAN PUREE

YIELDS APPROXIMATELY 2 CUPS

Fava beans may seem like a bit of work since you need to peel the outer skin off the beans, but it is imperative to get the best flavor out of them. That outer skin is rather bitter and, for me, greatly affects the taste of this earthy-sweet bean. Be aware that there is a great waste percentage with fava beans since the shell tends to weigh more than the beans contained within. So, when buying them, feel along the pod to make sure there is a full allotment developed within.

4 cups fresh shelled fava beans (approx. $4\frac{1}{2}$ pounds in their pods)

$\frac{1}{2}$ cup truffle-infused oil

$\frac{1}{4}$ cup extra virgin olive oil

3 garlic cloves—chopped

$\frac{1}{4}$ cup savory leaves or thyme leaves—roughly chopped

Salt and black pepper to taste

Sourdough bread, toasted or grilled

Asiago or Pecorino cheese, shaved

Bring 4 cups of water to a boil and add the fava beans. Cook the beans at a rolling boil for about 5 minutes. Drain the beans in a colander and refresh under cold water to stop the cooking. Allow them to drain again. Peel the outer skin from the beans and discard.

Place the truffle-infused and olive oils, garlic, savory, salt, pepper, and flesh of the beans in a food processor or blender. Process to a smooth paste. Taste and correct seasoning.

Serve on toasted or grilled sourdough bread or your favorite bread with shaved Asiago or Pecorino cheese.

ARTICHOKE PUREE
YIELDS APPROXIMATELY 2 CUPS

Besides just enjoying this puree on crusty, lightly toasted bread, I like to use it as a sauce for pasta. To use it as a sauce, thin the puree with some olive oil and then toss with your favorite pasta, some tomatoes, yellow peppers, and freshly torn basil leaves. A word of advice if you use a blender to process this puree or any puree for that matter: always place all of the liquids in first. This helps start a strong-enough whirlpool action to draw the heavier solid materials toward the blender's blades.

½ pound artichoke hearts—frozen

4 pounds artichoke—fresh

1 garlic clove—roughly chopped

1 lemon—juiced

¼ cup mint leaves

⅛ cup Italian parsley

½ cup extra virgin olive oil

Salt and black pepper to taste

If using fresh artichoke hearts, precook them. Trim the thorny tops off, and place in a 3-quart pot and cover with water so the artichokes are floating in a couple inches of water. Place a small lid right on top of the artichokes to keep them submerged—they are buoyant. Bring to a boil over a medium heat—cooking for 15 minutes until fork-tender. Then peel away and discard the leaves and clean away the choke. The remaining bottom is the heart. If using frozen artichoke hearts, thaw and drain in a colander before using.

Place all of the ingredients in a food processor or blender and blend until smooth.

GRILLED SQUID SALAD

We all know the translucent watery mung bean sprouts that we've been finding tossed into our stir-fried dinners or as a component in a vegetarian brown rice and vegetable dish. As the saying goes, "they've come a long way . . . " and now there are a plethora of sprout possibilities coming from various beans and seeds. Sprouts should be stored in the refrigerator in a dry plastic bag that is not sealed closed. They should be crisp without signs of excess moisture or a musty smell. Use them within 3 to 4 days of purchase.

> 2 pounds squid—cleaned
>
> 4 stalks garlic—root discarded, sliced thinly
>
> 2 teaspoons salt
>
> 1 teaspoon black pepper
>
> 1 cup Sorrel Oil (page 50)
>
> ¼ pound mixed sprouts—such as buckwheat, snow pea, and sunflower

Heat a grill to very hot. Pat the squid dry and cut into 1-inch rings, keeping the legs whole. Toss the squid with the garlic, salt, and pepper, and let sit 15 minutes.

Grill the squid for about 3 minutes total, and as you pull the squid off the grill, place in a bowl with the sorrel oil. Then toss in the mixed sprouts and serve warm or cold.

Deep in a cupboard
Mysterious jars beckoning
The usages you'll know

MAIN COURSES

LAMB RAGOUT

YIELDS 6 SERVINGS

This quick-cooking ragout offers lots of flavor and great versatility. I toss it with gnocchi or penne pasta; or I treat it as a fancy "sloppy joe" over crusty peasant bread. This is also a good freezer item, which can be defrosted in the mircowave oven without the sauce losing any of its fabulous taste.

¼ cup olive oil

2 garlic cloves—chopped

1 tablespoon red chili flakes

2 bay leaves

½ pound coarsely ground lamb

¼ cup red wine

16-oz can, peeled whole tomatoes

2 red peppers—roasted, peeled, seeded, and julienned

1 pound spinach—washed and roughly torn

¼ cup black olives—pitted (such as Kalamata, nicoise or Gaeta)

¼ cup pine nuts—lightly toasted

½ cup Parmesan cheese—grated

Salt and black pepper to taste

Heat a bottom-lined, 2-quart sauté pan to hot, and add the olive oil. Cook the garlic cloves, chili flakes, and bay leaves for 3 minutes. Add the ground lamb, stirring, until browned, about 3-5 minutes. Pour in the wine and reduce for about 3 minutes until syrupy. Mix in the tomatoes and peppers and bring to a boil. Reduce the heat to a simmer and cook for 30 minutes. Mix in remaining ingredients and cook an additional 10 minutes. Correct the seasoning and serve over your favorite pasta.

LAMB MARINATED
IN TROPICAL JUICE

YIELDS 4 TO 6 SERVINGS

The lamb used in this recipe is a boneless loin roast. In Australia and New Zealand this is a typical cut, but in the States, you must ask your butcher for a New Zealand cut lamb. The beauty of the lamb loin fillet is that there should be no fat or grizzle to trim. This recipe is unusual because the marinating process occurs after the meat has been cooked, which is typical in many authentic Spanish, Italian, and Caribbean dishes.

6 to 8 lamb loin fillets (approx. 2¼ pounds)

2 teaspoons white pepper

2 tablespoons sesame oil

2 to 3 garlic cloves—crushed to bruised

8 mint stems—use the leaves for another purpose

1 cup unsweetened guava or papaya juice

2 cups red wine

Salt

1 pound spinach or 1½ pounds baby bok choy

Extra virgin olive oil

Season the lamb with white pepper. Heat the sesame oil to hot in a 12-inch sauté pan. Sear the lamb on all sides, cooking for a total of 7 to 8 minutes. The lamb should be rare. Transfer the lamb to a plate.

Add the garlic cloves, mint stems, juice, wine, and salt to the hot sauté pan. Bring to a boil and reduce to a simmer. Cook the mixture for 5 minutes. Then cool the mixture.

Place the lamb and the marinade in an airtight container and refrigerate for 6 hours or over overnight.

Serve the lamb sliced thin over a bed of chilled steamed spinach or baby bok choy and a drizzle of extra virgin olive oil. Cook the spinach by placing it in boiling water for 30 seconds and then drain. Baby bok choy needs to be cooked for 2 minutes in boiling water, and then drained. This dish makes a fabulous cold first course or an elegant lunch entrée. It will keep refrigerated for up to 1 week in its marinade.

GRILL PLATE

YIELDS 6 SERVINGS

Spring is the time to scrub the grill grate, replace the lava stones on your gas barbecue, break out the tongs, and grill, grill, grill. I love to grill underripe fruits (such as peaches, plums, apricots, and pears as the season moves on) and present them as a savory item. For portobello mushrooms, I recommend cutting out the gills before grilling, since they contain a lot of moisture and tend to leach out an unattractive brown juice. Though never fear if you do not have a grill, you can roast all the items in a 475°F oven until just tender, about 5 minutes.

¼ cup summer savory leaves—roughly chopped (or use a mix of thyme and parsley)

1 cup olive oil

1½ pounds asparagus—washed and trimmed

3 portobello mushrooms—halved, gills removed

2 pounds fully cooked smoked sausage (any brand)—cut on an angle

Infuse the savory in the oil by warming in a 2-cup saucepan over a very low heat for 15 minutes. Don't let the oil boil for you or you'll fry the herb. Heat the grill to very hot. Brush all ingredients with the infused oil and grill. The asparagus will take about 5 minutes; the portobello mushroom will take 8 to 10 minutes; and the sausage just needs to be warmed through. Lightly brush with the remaining infused oil after removing from the grill and serve.

TUNA WITH ROSEMARY

YIELDS 8 SERVINGS

In Tokyo's Shiji Market I witnessed the tuna auction. This daily ritual was the highlight of the market. I was amazed by all the hoopla surrounding this hour-long buying frenzy. Competition for prime positioning at the auction block was downright aggressive and the bidding fierce with the day's top fish selling for hundreds of dollars. Needless to say, the Japanese take their tuna very seriously, with never a thought that it should end up canned, bathed in oil, or tossed with mayonnaise pressed between two starchy sheets.

1 lemon—juiced

¼ cup extra virgin olive oil

¼ cup rosemary leaves—roughly chopped

2 tablespoons Italian parsley leaves—roughly chopped

2 garlic cloves—minced

½ cup plain bread crumbs

Salt and black pepper to taste

3 pounds Tuna—cut into eight pieces

½ cup dry white wine

Mix the lemon juice, olive oil, rosemary, parsley, garlic cloves, bread crumbs, and salt and pepper together. Pat the mixture onto both sides of each piece of tuna, and place in a baking dish. Refrigerate for 30 minutes.

Preheat the oven to 375°F.

Drizzle the wine over the tuna and place in the oven. Bake the tuna for approximately 10 minutes and serve immediately over a bed of Wilted Escarole Scented with Garlic (page 33).

Notes

This recipe bucks the trend to serve tuna fillets rare. Though I will admit that I only like my sushi raw, when I cook tuna, I prefer it medium to medium well. If you are fond of rare tuna, cut the cooking time on the recipe by a few minutes. When buying tuna, look for firm flesh that has an even, dark red hue and no white connective tissue running through it.

STEAMERS WITH WILD RAMPS

YIELDS 6 TO 8 SERVINGS

Notes

When cleaning steamers, do not submerge them in water or you'll lose all their wonderful flavors. The best way to clean clams is to scrub them with a stiff brush under cold running water.

Discovering these relatives of the lily family was one of those moments of culinary awe. I found their garlicky-onion flavor mild but when I spoke to a chef who grew up in West Virginia, her memory of ramps was that of a very strong-flavored vegetable. For me this difference represents how soil and weather conditions under which something grows can greatly affect its flavor. Chili peppers are a clear example of this: the further into warmer climates you go, the hotter the chilies tend to get. The lesson here is that flavors of locally grown foods will vary depending on the region in which you live.

12 ramps (or substitute young leeks or scallions)

1 cup white wine

70 steamers—washed to discard any sand clinging to the shells

½ cup water

2 tablespoons olive oil

2 tablespoons unsalted butter

Black pepper to taste

Peasant bread, freshly sliced

Trim the root base from the ramps and wash them well, since there tends to be a fair amount of dirt clinging to the base. Pat dry. Cut the green top from the white base. Roughly chop both, but keep them separate.

In a high-sided 10-inch saucepan large enough to comfortably accommodate all of the steamers and still have a lid fit snugly, place the white wine and chopped ramp whites. Cover the pan and simmer on a low flame for 30 minutes. Add the steamers, ramp greens, water, oil, butter, and black pepper. Cover the pan and simmer for 15 minutes, or until the steamers have opened. Serve immediately with crusty peasant bread slices for dipping in the cooking liquid.

BLISTERED ASPARAGUS

YIELDS 6 SERVINGS

I adore asparagus so much that I fantasize about following spring across the globe to continually capture one of her finest offerings. Try to find the young, pencil-thin asparagus. They are less fibrous than their older brethren and have a more delicate flavor.

1½ pound asparagus

¼ cup olive oil

Coarse salt—such as kosher or sea salt

Freshly ground black pepper to taste

Juice of 1 lemon

4 ounces goat cheese—crumbled

Preheat the oven to 450°F.

Trim the base of the asparagus and wash well under cold running water. Pat the asparagus dry and then toss to coat with the oil.

Line a baking tray with parchment paper and lay out the asparagus in a single layer. Sprinkle with salt and black pepper to taste. Roast in the oven for 5 to 10 minutes, depending on the thickness of the asparagus. The pencil-thin asparagus usually need to cook only 5 minutes.

Transfer the asparagus to a serving platter, sprinkle with the crumbled goat cheese, and drizzle with lemon juice.

Notes

Trimming asparagus takes on two different techniques. If they are the pencil-thin ones, you should simply line them up and lop off the bottoms about 2 inches from the base. If they are the thicker ones, you want to gently snap the stalk near the base. I tend to snap a few to start with and then use those as my guide to trim the remaining asparagus. Line them up at the tips for this and then cut off the base.

Tender tip piercing
Tight green leaves beckoning us
Tended in our gardens

SAUTÉED RAMPS

YIELDS 6 SERVINGS

This wild onion is another harbinger of warmer weather, since it's one of the first vegetables to come to market in the spring. They're only available for about 1 month, but young leeks can easily be substituted. These onions have a gentle garlicky-onion flavor and can be eaten raw or cooked. Like a scallion, the entire plant is used. Trim the roots and wash away any dirt. Look for dark green, broad leaves. Use them through the spring in lieu of leeks or scallions.

24 ramps

½ cup champagne vinegar

¾ cup water

2 tablespoons Dijon mustard

½ cup olive oil

Salt and black pepper to taste

To clean the ramps, cut off the root base and wash under running water to dislodge any dirt—particularly where all the leaves gather toward the bottom. Pat dry.

Heat a 12-inch sauté pan to very hot, and add a tablespoon of the olive oil. Place the ramps in the pan in a single layer, and sauté to lightly colored, about 4-5 minutes. Reduce the heat to medium-low. Add the champagne vinegar and water, and cook for 10 more minutes. Transfer the ramps to a platter. In the sauté pan, whisk in the mustard and salt and pepper. Remove the pan from the heat and whisk in the remaining oil. Then drizzle the warm sauce over the ramps. Serve either hot or at room temperature.

FRIED GREEN TOMATOES

YIELDS 8 SERVINGS

Notes

The tomatoes should be just submerged in the oil when cooking so there should be no necessity to flip them over. If they are not just covered by the oil, add a little more, since the less you handle them the less likely they are to fall apart.

Where to start on the topic of tomatoes? There has been such an explosion of heirloom varieties over the past few years that our choices have grown twenty-plus-fold. Tomatoes today range in color from variegated green to yellow to orange to the familiar red. From the size of a currant to the size of a softball. I say try them all! The tomatoes used in this recipe are your standard beefsteak, which are underripe with a slightly sour taste, though make sure you leave enough to ripen on the vine. There is nothing more simply sublime than a summer plate of ripe tomatoes sliced, sprinkled with sea salt, and drizzled with fabulous extra virgin olive oil.

1½ pound green tomatoes (underripe tomatoes)

2 cups cornmeal

2 teaspoons salt

1 teaspoon black pepper

1½ cups Dijon mustard

½ cup canola oil

Wash and the dry the tomatoes. Slice them into ½-inch thick rounds. Mix the cornmeal, salt, and pepper together. Using a pastry brush, liberally coat the tomatoes with Dijon mustard and dredge them in the cornmeal mix, lightly patting the mixture into the tomatoes.

Heat a 12-inch skillet and place about 1-inch of oil in the pan and heat to hot. Add the tomatoes, in small batches, cooking for about 4 minutes or until golden brown. The oil should sizzle as soon as you lay the tomatoes in; otherwise it is too cool and will cause you to have greasy, heavy-tasting fried tomatoes. Once golden brown, transfer the tomatoes to paper towels to drain. Serve immediately, or keep warm in a 175°F oven for about 1 hour.

WILTED ESCAROLE
SCENTED WITH GARLIC
YIELDS 4 SERVINGS

I remember as a kid enjoying a particular canned soup that contained escarole and rice. For any Italian this is probably a rather common soup, but for me it was the height of sophistication and was a favorite after-school snack. Walking through the Wednesday Santa Monica market, I rediscovered this slightly bitter green. Big, bushy, and dusted with dark, rich-looking soil—as an adult I haven't lost my taste for escarole one bit.

1 pound escarole

¼ cup olive oil

3 garlic cloves—sliced paperthin

Salt and black pepper to taste

Trim the root base from the escarole and wash well. Drain in a colander to allow some of the water to drip off.

Heat a 12-inch sauté pan to hot and add the oil. Sauté the escarole adding a quarter of the escarole at a time. Halfway through, toss in the garlic and continue to add the remaining escarole. Cook the escarole just until it's wilted, about 5 minutes. Season with salt and pepper and serve immediately.

WILTED GREENS WITH COCONUT

YIELDS 4 SERVINGS

I lived in Australia for a couple of years, and my palate has never been the same. I grew to enjoy the intermingling of sweet, sour, and salty flavors as well as the mix of slightly bitter with sweet in a savory dish. If you do not have access to a coconut tree to make your own shaved fresh coconut (and how many of us do?), head to any Indian or Southeast Asian market to find unsweetened coconut.

> **2 tablespoons sesame oil**
>
> **2 pounds greens—such as spinach, bok choy, or Chinese broccoli, washed well**
>
> **¼ cup unsweetened shredded coconut**
>
> **Salt and black pepper to taste**

Heat a 12-inch sauté pan or wok to hot, and add the oil. Cook the greens until just wilted, then add the coconut and toss to combine. Season with salt and pepper. Depending on what greens you decide to use will determine the cooking time. Spinach takes about 3 minutes where Chinese broccoli will take at least 5 minutes. Serve immediately.

BARLEY WITH CARAMELIZED ONIONS AND MUSHROOMS

YIELDS 6 SERVINGS

The flavor of this nutty-earthy grain sends me back to my childhood and steaming bowls of my mother's famous mushroom barely soup. Here is a side dish that will pair fantastically with a roast, grilled fish, or a melody of vegetables. Or try this recipe as a stuffing for a whole chicken.

2 medium Vidalia onions

3 tablespoons olive oil

2 garlic cloves—diced

¼ pound wild mushrooms—cleaned and sliced thin

2 tablespoons thyme—leaves only

3 cups chicken stock (homemade or canned, low-sodium)

1 cup pearl barley

Salt and black pepper to taste

Slice the onions into very thin julienne strips. Heat a 2-quart saucepan over medium heat and add the oil. Add the onions and cook until golden, approximately 15 to 20 minutes, tossing constantly so the onions don't burn. Add the garlic and wild mushrooms and continue cooking for another 5 minutes. Add the thyme leaves and slowly pour in the chicken stock. Bring to a boil and then add the barley. Season with salt and pepper. Cover and reduce the temperature to low, simmering for another 20 to 25 minutes. Turn off the heat and let rest for 10 minutes, then fluff the barley with a fork. Serve warm.

ROASTED ARTICHOKES

YIELDS 4 SERVINGS

Artichokes have always been one of my favorite foods. I remember the jars of marinated artichoke hearts my mother would buy so I would have them for my after-school salad (yes, I was a strange child). Today, I occasionally eat that childhood treat. But I reserve my indulgence until spring and then again in late autumn when artichokes once again appear. I am partial to the small baby artichokes. These tend not to have a well-developed choke, offering an easier eat. Always buy artichokes that have tightly compact bodies and are dense to the touch, with no black bruising.

> 16 to 20 baby artichokes or 32-ounce can whole artichokes in water—drained
>
> 2 lemons—zested and juiced (1 lemon just cut in half for rubbing on the artichoke)
>
> ¼ cup olive oil
>
> 1 small red onion—julienned
>
> 1 small carrot—diced
>
> ½ cup balsamic vinegar
>
> ⅛ cup pine nuts—lightly toasted
>
> 1 bunch Italian parsley—leaves only, chopped (approx. ½ cup)
>
> Salt and black pepper to taste

If using fresh baby artichokes, prepare them by peeling away the bottom leaves and trimming the base to expose the whitish flesh. Rub all places where you have made a cut with some lemon to prevent browning. Cut off the top of the artichokes to remove the thorny leaves and then rub with lemon. In a four-quart pot filled with enough water to cover the artichokes, add the juice of a lemon and the artichokes and bring to a boil. Lay a plate over the artichokes to keep them submerged in the water. This will help prevent them from browning. Simmer for 20 minutes or until tender. Drain and cool.

Preheat the oven to 450°F.

Coat a roasting tray with the olive oil, and spread the artichokes in a single layer out onto the tray. Put in the oven, and roast for 10 minutes. Add the onion and carrot and roast for another 10 minutes. Remove the roasting tray from the oven, and immediately transfer them to a mixing bowl. While still hot, mix in the balsamic vinegar, pine nuts, parsley, lemon zest, and salt and pepper. Toss well, and serve either hot or cold.

BOCCONCINI SALAD

YIELDS 6 TO 8 SERVINGS

Bocconcini means "little mouth full" and refers to the size of the moz-zarella cheese. If you cannot find the smaller-shaped bocconcini, just use mozzarella cheese cut into 1-inch cubes. It is most important when making a salad like this that you don't add any kind of acid to the mix. Vinegar or lemon juice will cause the tender cheese to toughen and become rather chewy. The lemon zest and sorrel used in this recipe will give the salad a bit of piquancy.

> 1 pound bocconcini—small mozzarella balls
>
> Zest of 1 lemon—diced
>
> ¼ cup capers—rinsed, drained, and roughly chopped
>
> ¼ cup Italian parsley—leaves only, chopped
>
> 2 cups arugula—washed, dried, and roughly chopped
>
> 1 cup sorrel leaves—washed, dried, and roughly chopped
>
> 1 medium-sized red pepper—seeded and diced
>
> ½ cup Kalamata olives—pitted and roughly chopped
>
> Black pepper to taste
>
> ½ cup extra virgin olive oil

Toss all ingredients together and let sit 30 minutes before serving to allow the flavors to blend well.

DESSERTS

STRAWBERRY COMPOTE WITH HOMEMADE RICOTTA CHEESE

YIELDS 6 SERVINGS

Ricotta cheese is the simplest of cheeses to make, and now that I'm past my fear of using my alchemist power to create these sweet curds, I find the commercial variety a letdown. Regular milk is fine, but I tend to get fresh goat's milk at the farmer's market. It makes for a slightly tarter version of cheese.

Ricotta cheese

2 quarts whole milk or fresh goat's milk

½ cup distilled white vinegar

In a 4-quart saucepan, bring the milk to just below the boiling point, approximately 180°F, and remove from the heat. Stir in the vinegar, giving the milk about three stirs only. Allow the mixture to sit for 20 to 25 minutes at room temperature. The milk should start to curdle almost immediately. If it does not start to curdle within the first 5 minutes, add another ¼ cup of vinegar.

Line a sieve with about 4 to 5 layers of cheesecloth and place over a deep bowl or pot. Gently pour the curds and whey into the sieve. Allow the cheese to sit for 30 minutes to drain off the whey. The curds are your ricotta. Use immediately or refrigerate for a few days. You should store the ricotta in a glass bowl with a piece of plastic placed right down on top of it to prevent a skin from forming.

Strawberry Compote

1 quart strawberries

¼ cup honey

¼ cup lemon balm—leaves only, roughly chopped (or use mint, hyssop, or lavender)

With a damp towel, wipe the strawberries clean of any dirt. Cut off the green tops from the strawberries, known as the hull. Then cut the strawberries in half or quarters, depending on their size.

In a 2-quart saucepan large enough to hold all of the ingredients, add half of the strawberries, the honey, and lemon balm. Cook the strawberries over a medium flame until they just start to break down, approximately 15 minutes. Then mix in the remaining strawberries and remove from the heat.

To serve, place a dollop of the ricotta on the plate and cover with a spoonful of the strawberry compote. Garnish with a crisp almond cookie.

RHUBARB AND ALMOND CRISP

YIELDS 8 SERVINGS

Rhubarb for me is one of those very familiar fruits of spring. When I was growing up in the era of canned foods galore, fresh rhubarb somehow was one of fruits my mom used in her fruit pie—I guess it was not available canned. This fruit is not a New World native at all; it is believed to have originated in northern China and eastern Siberia. Regardless of its homeland, this tart, red stalk is a welcomed addition to my springtime tableau.

2 pounds fresh rhubarb—cut into 1-inch pieces (or 2 pounds frozen)

¾ cup sugar

½ cup dried apricots—chopped

½ cup dried cherries

2 teaspoons vanilla extract

Crisp Topping

¾ pound cold unsalted butter

1¼ cup rolled oats

½ cup brown sugar

½ cup all-purpose flour

½ cup slivered almonds

In a 4-quart saucepan, add the rhubarb and sugar and cook over a medium heat until the rhubarb starts to break down, about 10 to 15 minutes. Mix in the apricots, cherries, and vanilla extract and remove from the heat.

To make the crisp topping, cut the butter into small pieces. Place all the remaining ingredients in a large bowl, add the butter, and with two forks (or your fingertips), cut the butter into the flour mixture until it resembles a coarse meal.

Preheat the oven to 350°F.

In 8 6-ounce ovenproof ramekins, equally divide the rhubarb-mixture filling and then sprinkle the crisp topping over the fruit. Bake for 30 minutes until the top is set and golden.

STRAWBERRY SHORTCAKES

YIELDS 8 SERVINGS

Notes
You can make the shortcake dough in a food processor fitted with a plastic blade. Add all the dry ingredients into the food processor and then, with an on/off pulse, combine the ingredients. Then add in the cut butter, and, again using an on/off pulse, mix to resemble a coarse meal. With the machine running, pour in the cream, and as soon as it starts to pull together, stop the machine. Just be aware that this technique moves quickly, so pay attention.

Having lived in Australia where British customs still hold fast, I enjoyed many an afternoon tea. There is a service called *Devonshire Tea* where, along with a pot of dark black brew, one gets freshly made scones, clotted cream, and strawberry jam. All I ever imagined during this moment were strawberry shortcakes and wondered if this was not the genesis of that classic sweet.

Shortcakes

2 cups all-purpose flour

½ teaspoon salt

1 tablespoon baking powder

2 tablespoons sugar

1 teaspoon cinnamon—ground

4 ounces unsalted butter—cut into small pieces

1 cup cream

2 tablespoons cream—for brushing the top of the cakes

Preheat the oven to 450°F.

Mix the flour, salt, baking powder, sugar, and cinnamon together. Cut the butter into the flour until the mixture resembles a coarse meal. It is all right if there are a few larger pieces of butter remaining. Add the cream, mixing to moisten the flour mixture. Turn the dough out onto a lightly floured board and knead a few times to bring it together. Be sure not to overwork the dough or it will make the shortcake tough and dry. Roll the dough out to a ½ inch-thick circle. Cut out 3-inch rounds or whatever shape you like. Collect the scraps, roll out, and cut out remaining shapes. Place the shortbread cakes on a parchment-lined baking tray. Brush the tops of the cakes with the 2 tablespoons of cream, and then place in the oven. Bake for 10 to 12 minutes until lightly browned.

Strawberries

4 pints strawberries—hulled and quartered

1 cup fresh orange juice

1 cup sugar

Mix the strawberries, orange juice, and sugar and set aside.

Whipped Cream

2 cups cream

¼ cup superfine sugar

Whip the 2 cups of cream with the superfine sugar until they form soft peaks.

To assemble, split the shortcake in half. Place a small dollop of whipped cream on the plate and put the shortcake base on the cream. Then dollop some more whipped cream and a heaping tablespoon of strawberries onto the shortcake and then some more whipped cream. Place the top of the shortcakes on that layer of whipped cream, add another spoonful of strawberries and add a final dollop of whipped cream.

RHUBARB AND STRAWBERRY COBBLER

YIELDS 8 SERVINGS

This cobbler recipe takes me through the seasons. In the summer I am likely to slice peaches and toss them in with pitted cherries, a squeeze of lemon juice, and some sugar. Avoid precooking the peach filling first or it will break down too much. Come autumn, I use pears with almonds as my filling. The pears *do* need to cook for about 5 to 10 minutes in some butter, sugar, and, if you feel so inclined, a tasteful splash of amaretto (almond-flavored liqueur). I do tend to make cobbler in individual servings as I am not a fan of the way it looks when cut up and served on a plate. Any ovenproof serving containers will do. If I am making one large cobbler, I will serve the dessert at the table so the beauty of the dish can be seen. If fresh lavender flowers are found in your market, substitute 2 teaspoons of them for the mint in the rhubarb, for an unusual floral moment.

Rhubarb Strawberry Filling

2 pounds rhubarb—washed and cut into 1-inch pieces (or 2 pounds frozen)

½ cup sugar

¼ cup water

2 pints strawberries—hull removed and cut in half

½ cup diced dried fruit—such as apricots, pineapples, and cherries

¼ cup mint leaves—chopped

In a four-quart saucepan add the rhubarb, sugar, and the water. Simmer over medium heat for 10 minutes, stirring every so often. Then mix in the strawberries, dried fruit, and mint and simmer another 5 minutes. Remove from the heat and let sit for 10 minutes. Transfer the rhubarb mixture to a 8 x 8 x 2 baking dish or into 8 6-ounce individual ramekins.

Cobbler Topping

2 cups all-purpose flour

2 tablespoons sugar

½ teaspoon nutmeg

¾ teaspoon baking soda

1½ teaspoons baking powder

¼ teaspoon salt

5 tablespoon unsalted butter—chilled

½ cup buttermilk

½ cup cream

½ teaspoon vanilla extract

To prepare the cobbler topping combine the flour, sugar, nutmeg, baking soda, baking powder, and salt in a large mixing bowl. With two forks (or your fingertips), cut the butter into the flour mixture, until it resembles coarse meal. In a separate bowl whisk the buttermilk, cream, and vanilla extract. Add it to the flour mixture and blend until it resembles a sticky dough.

Preheat the oven to 375°F.

Spoon the cobbler topping over the rhubarb mixture. Sprinkle additional sugar if desired, and bake uncovered for about 25 minutes or until the top is golden brown. Serve warm or cold with a dollop of whipped cream or a scoop of vanilla ice cream.

LAVENDER RICOTTA CAKE

YIELDS 8 SERVINGS

Yes, I confess I am in love with lavender. It is one of those fragrances that transports me to languid, sun-drenched days. I was amazed when I learned it had culinary applications and immediately set out to play with it. When cooking with lavender, use judicious amounts or it can take on too floral an aroma, which to some can taste "soapy."

Crust

> **20 amaretti cookies (Italian hard-almond cookies)**
>
> **¼ cup finely ground almonds**
>
> **1 cup shredded sweetened coconut**
>
> **2 egg whites—lightly beaten**

Preheat the oven to 350°F.

In a food processor fitted with a steel blade, grind the cookies to a fine meal. Transfer the ground cookies to a workbowl and mix in the ground almonds, shredded coconut, and lightly beaten egg whites. Work the mixture together so when pressed, it will hold together. Press the crust mixture into an 8-inch springform cake pan, making sure to come just slightly up the sides of the pan. Place the pan in the oven and bake for 7 minutes, or until the crust is set and slightly golden. Remove from the oven and cool completely.

Filling

> **2 pounds ricotta cheese**
>
> **6 whole eggs—beaten**
>
> **2 teaspoons dried lavender**
>
> **½ cup honey**

Prepare the filling, thoroughly mixing together the ricotta, eggs, lavender, and honey.

Preheat the oven to 325°F.

Pour the ricotta mixture into the prepared crust and place in the middle rack of the oven. Bake for 30 to 40 minutes or until set. Shut off the oven and let the cake cool in the oven for about 45 minutes. Remove from the oven and place on a rack, allowing the cake to cool completely. Carefully remove the springform and serve this cake with fresh seasonal berries and lavender sprigs.

LAVENDER TUILES

YIELDS APPROXIMATELY 20 COOKIES

These little cookies can take an ordinary scoop of vanilla ice cream and elevate it to heights you never thought possible. So very delicate, these cookies last no longer than 48 hours or they'll become too soft. So, eat them all up while you can. Serve with fresh berries and a dollop of freshly made ricotta cheese.

> 4 ounces unsalted butter—at room temperature
>
> ½ cup sugar
>
> Zest of ½ orange—finely diced
>
> 2 teaspoons orange blossom water
>
> 2 egg whites
>
> ¼ cup plus 1 tablespoon all-purpose flour
>
> 2 teaspoons lavender

Preheat the oven to 350°F.

In a bowl, beat the butter and sugar until it becomes a smooth whitened mass. Beat in the zest and orange blossom water and then the egg whites, one at a time, making sure the batter is smooth before adding the second egg white. You can use a standing mixer or a hand-held beater for this process. Add the flour and lavender, by hand, stirring to thoroughly incorporate. Adding the flour by hand prevents the cookie from getting overworked and tough.

Flip a baking tray over and butter and flour it. It is easier to remove the cookies if the lip of the tray does not prevent you from getting a good angle with your spatula. Place a tablespoon of the batter onto the tray and spread it out very thin. Bake the cookies for 8 to 10 minutes or until golden and firm. Remove immediately from the baking tray onto a cooling rack. The cookies go from golden to burnt very quickly and every oven is a bit different, so pay close attention.

Store in an airtight container.

VINEGARS AND OILS

STRAWBERRY VINAIGRETTE
YIELDS APPROXIMATELY 2 CUPS

If a vinaigrette could be considered sexy, then this is the one. The pale mauve color created by the strawberries seduces the eye and its sweet tartness dances across your tongue. This is an easy way to get fruit flavor into a vinegar without making your own vinegar. You can use this technique throughout the seasons with raspberries, plums, peaches, or kiwis, as they become available. Dress a salad of arugula or a grilled chicken breast with this dressing.

½ cup roughly chopped strawberries (cleaned and hulled)

¼ cup champagne vinegar or white wine vinegar

1 tablespoon dijon mustard

Salt and black pepper to taste

1 cup almond or canola oil

Place the strawberries and the vinegar in the blender and process until smooth. Pass this strawberry/vinegar mixture through a fine mesh sieve over a large bowl to remove the seeds. Add the mustard, salt, and pepper, whisking constantly to thoroughly mix. Then slowly drizzle in the oil, whisk to thoroughly combine and emulsify.

SORREL OIL

I have a thing for lemon-scented foods, and sorrel leaves give me a happy pucker. This oblong leaf, visually reminiscent of a spinach leaf, has a terrific sour taste that is at home torn in a salad mix, applied as an herb, or quickly wilted as a leafy green. The sorrel oil being made in this recipe will successfully dress most fish dishes and is a great marinade base for poultry. Make extra sorrel oil and store it in the freezer for up to 6 months.

½ cup canola oil

½ cup almond oil (or use canola oil)

¼ pound sorrel leaves—washed, dried, and ribs removed

2 teaspoons salt

2 teaspoons freshly ground black pepper

In a blender place the oils, sorrel, salt, and pepper. Process until smooth.

Use with Grilled Squid Salad (page 22), as a marinade, or as a garnish for Chilled Cucumber Mint Soup (page 72).

NOTES

NOTES

NOTES

SUMMER

Morning dew clings everywhere
Clothes on the line gone limp
Rubied jewels fresh from the fields—waiting

❧ SUMMER'S BOUNTY ❧

Who cannot be seduced by the plethora of vegetables, fruits, and herbs available during this season? It is a particularly special time of year for the majority of us who live in regions of the country that suffer through the chilling sleep of winter. The lucky denizens of the southern portion of the United States will find that some of these offerings are available to them year-round.

Vegetables	Herbs	Fruits
Avocado	Basil	Apricots
Almonds	Bay laurel	Blackberries
Beans	Chamomile	Blueberries
Beets	Chives	Boysenberries
Broccoli	Cilantro	Cherries
Burdock	Dill	Currants
Cabbage	Garlic	Figs
Carrots	Lavender	Gooseberries
Celery	Lemon balm	Grapes
Chayote squash	Marjoram	Guava
Chili peppers	Mint	Mangoes
Collards	Oregano	Melons
Corn	Rosemary	Nectarines
Cucumbers	Sage	Papayas
Diakon	Savory	Peaches
Eggplant	Spearmint	Plums
Fennel	Tarragon	Raspberries
Husk tomatoes	Texas tarragon (Mexican mint)	Watermelon

Vegetables

Jicama

Kale

Kohlrabi

Lima beans

Okra

Onions

Patty pan squash

Peas

Peppers

Potatoes

Raddicchio

Radishes

Tomatillios

Tomato

Shallots

Sugar snap peas

Snake squash

Turnips (baby)

Zucchini

Imagine the pre-Columbian world where peppercorns were the primary source of heat in a dish. So prompted the journey of Columbus west in hopes of finding a quicker route to the Spice Islands (for clove, nutmeg, and mace) and the Malabar Coast of India (for peppercorns). We all know what happened to Columbus. This "New World" found a new plant that offered heat and was called a pepper. The heat in a pepper ranges from incendiary to mild to sweet. When dealing with the hotter varieties, some precautions should be taken. Either wear surgical gloves or drizzle some oil over the pepper before chopping. The oil will prevent the capsaicin, which is the enzyme that creates that burning sensation, from getting trapped in the oils of your fingers. As a matter of fact, it is a nerve receptor in the back of the throat that registers the pleasing hot flavor experience of the pepper. Conversely, the same type of nerve endings located in the eye does not perceive the pepper as a good taste, but purely as pain. The seeds and membrane of the pepper contain the highest concentrations of the enzyme, so discarding them helps lower the heat level of the pepper. The pepper's heat level increases when it is dried, due to the absence of water and the concentration of the capsaicin.

A great way to preserve peppers is to make pastes with them and have them all winter long. For example, take Thai chilies and sauté them with garlic in sesame oil until they blister. Then place the chilies and oil into a blender and process till smooth—this makes what is called *sambal*. Go Latin with habanero peppers and blend them with some cooked carrots, onion, garlic, tamarind paste, and cumin seeds. This habanero blend makes a good base for a jerk marinade. All you need do is add some scallions, parsley, and thyme and then spread it on your meat. One word of warning: When blending any peppers, the capsaicin becomes airborne and can be very irritating. Make sure the room is well-ventilated and/or wear a surgical mask.

To prepare roasted peppers: Preheat your oven to 350° to 400°F. Rub the peppers with a little olive oil and place them on a baking tray in the oven. Turn the peppers occasionally, allowing them to blister on all sides. This should take about 20 minutes. Alternatively, if you have a gas range, place the peppers directly on the burner grate over the open flame, turning them to blacken all over. When the peppers are charred, remove from the oven or the burner grate and place in a sealed plastic bag or a covered bowl. Let the peppers sit for 15 minutes to allow the skin to steam away from the flesh. Remove from the bag and rub the skin off with a paper towel. Cut in half and remove the seeds.

Chili Pepper Variety	Heat Level	Uses
Anaheim	Mild	Great to stuff, batter, and fry. Roast, seed, and skin, and add to grain dishes.
Cascabella	Incendiary . . . be careful	Add into pickles, or used dried in many Mexican sauces.
Cayenne	Hot	Primarily used dried—add in sparing amounts to a dish, since the flavor will develop during cooking.
Habanero	Explosive!	One of the hottest chilies on earth. Used very judiciously, it has great flavor along with its heat. Look for a chocolate variety.
Hungarian Wax	Mild	Great for pickling or stuffing.
Jalapeño	Hot to hotter	In the summer, the heat level of this pepper is at its most intense. Probably the best known of the American chilies with great versatility. When dried and smoked they become known as chipotle.

Pasilla	Mild	Used in Mexico's famed *mole* sauce. Add it into a tomato sauce for some extra zing.
Poblano	Mild	When dried, it becomes known as a ancho. A must for chili con carne. Or roast them and add them to a vegetable salad.
Serrano	Very hot	Great in pickles and salsas. A must in a guacamole.
Thai chili	Very hot	Also known as bird's-eye chili. Used in all Southeast Asian dishes.

❧ PUTTING UP VINEGARS AND OILS ❧

When putting up vinegars, you want to make sure you wash and dry the herbs, fruit, or vegetables and place them in a vinegar that will support their flavor. For example, I would use red wine vinegar for rosemary, garlic, chilies, mint, and oregano because the flavors of these items can stand up to the strength of the red wine vinegar. The gentler herbs such as dill, hyssop, or lemon grass do best in milder flavored vinegars. When I put up fruit vinegars, I tend to use cider, rice, white wine, or champagne vinegars to capture their flavor. The sweetness of the fruits for me seems best suited for these milder-flavored vinegars. It will take about 1 week for the flavor to infuse into the vinegar, which you should store in a cool, dark place.

The same is basically true for oils. Extra virgin olive oil will add its flavor agenda to whatever is being steeped in it. My tendency is to work with grape, canola, and almond oils since my infusions for these are flavorless to mildly sweet. In any recipe calling for these oils, you can easily replace one with the other. Also, it is important to store your infused oils in the refrigerator to prevent any anaerobic bacteria from developing and contaminating your hard work. If the oil coagulates in the refrigerator, this is not a problem. Just let it sit at room temperature for 15 minutes until it becomes completely liquid again. The process of chilling the oil and then returning it to room temperature does not destroy the integrity of the oil at all.

STARTERS

STRAWBERRY TOMATO SALSA

YIELDS APPROXIMATELY 2 CUPS

Who can resist the seductive scarlet cry of the strawberry? But for those of us who have succumbed to an untimely purchase, we were surely let down. I always eat one before I purchase the pint to make certain they are sweet and juicy. (Though don't let the manager catch you!) Do not buy strawberries with what is called "white shoulders"—where the area around the hull is whitish green. This almost guarantees a lackluster experience.

1 tomato—cut in half, seeds discarded

1 habanero pepper—seeded

1 small red onion—finely diced

1 scallion—finely minced

1 pint strawberries—washed, dried, hulled, and quartered

1 tablespoon fresh thyme—leaves only

2 teaspoons fresh oregano—leaves only

1 tablespoon sherry vinegar

1 tablespoon olive oil

Salt and black pepper to taste

Dice the tomato into a ¼ inch dice. Chop the habanero chili pepper very fine. Be careful not to let the inside flesh of the chili touch your hands, since the oils in this chili, as in most, are very potent. Put these in a large bowl and add the onion, scallion, and strawberries. Roughly chop the herbs and toss them into the bowl. Finally, add the vinegar and olive oil, salt and pepper, and mix well. Refrigerate the salsa 1 hour before serving. This salsa, as with many such fresh fruit salsas, has only a 1-day shelf life.

Notes

Salsas are a fantastic summertime sauce when the thought of lighting the stove sends you running to the pool. Best of all, clean up is minimal. However, they are very perishable, and therefore I make and eat my salsas on the same day. At best, most salsas will survive 24 hours.

MULTI-HERB PESTO

YIELDS APPROXIMATELY 3 CUPS

Pesto is an Italian word for paste and does not necessarily mean using only basil. All summer long, I blend my favorite herbs with simply enough oil to create a paste and store the pesto in the freezer. Then all autumn and winter long I have wonderful herbaceous reminders of summer's glory. As with most pestos, this condiment will last 1 month in the refrigerator or 6 months in the freezer. This pesto is superb with grilled meats or alternatively mixed with white wine vinegar for a flavorful vinaigrette.

1 cup watercress leaves—tightly packed

1 cup Italian parsley leaves—tightly packed

1 cup basil leaves—tightly packed

¼ cup thyme leaves—tightly packed

½ cup oregano leaves—tightly packed

½ cup macadamia nuts—chopped (or blanched almonds, pine nuts, or walnuts)

4 to 5 garlic cloves—roughly chopped

¼ cup Parmesan cheese—grated

¾ cup olive oil

Black pepper to taste

Wash the herbs and pat them dry. Pluck the leaves from their stems, making sure not to use any of the thicker woody stems, since they will not blend well.

Place the herbs and the remaining ingredients in a food processor. Blend until still fairly coarse.

CILANTRO-MINT PESTO

YIELDS APPROXIMATELY 3 CUPS

This is a great pesto with an Asian influence. The mint in this recipe helps balance the flavor of the cilantro and is worth a try if you are one of those people who swears off cilantro. I use it all summer over grilled foods, or I love to toss it with cold soba (Japanese buckwheat noodles).

2 cups cilantro leaves—tightly packed

1 cup mint leaves—tightly packed

2 tablespoons sesame seeds

$\frac{1}{2}$-inch long piece ginger root—peeled and diced

$\frac{1}{4}$ cup rice wine vinegar

1 tablespoon honey or brown sugar

$\frac{1}{2}$ cup low-sodium soy sauce

3 garlic cloves—crushed

2 teaspoons dry English mustard

Freshly ground black pepper to taste

$\frac{1}{8}$ teaspoon cayenne pepper

Wash the herbs to dislodge any dirt and debris, then pluck the leaves from their stems and pat dry. Place them in a food processor with the remaining ingredients and blend until smooth. Taste and correct seasoning with more black pepper and cayenne pepper, if necessary.

TOMATO SAUCE

YIELDS 4 CUPS

Notes

When cutting a tomato to remove the seeds, it is most efficient to cut the tomato through its circumference. The two halves will clearly expose the seed cavity and allow you quick work to discard them. Many recipes require you to seed the tomato because they can add a bitterness during the cooking process.

Freeze this sauce and in the dead of winter, pull it out as a remembrance of the abundance offered during the sun-soaked days of summer. You can also freeze fresh whole tomatoes as well and bring them out at a future date. Be aware that tomatoes that are frozen whole are suitable solely for sauces or soups, since the freezing/defrosting process causes them to break down and become very watery.

1 large yellow onion

4 pounds tomatoes (the beefsteak variety)—halved and seeds removed

1 tablespoon olive oil

4 sprigs of thyme (approx. 2 tablespoons)

2 garlic cloves—split in half

2 strips lemon zest

2 teaspoons honey

½ cup basil leaves—roughly chopped

Salt and black pepper to taste

Dice the onions and tomatoes. In a 6-quart saucepan, heat the oil over a medium heat and add the onions. Sauté until translucent, about 3 to 5 minutes, then add the tomatoes, thyme, and garlic. Cook for 20 minutes and then add the lemon zest and honey. Simmer for an additional 20 minutes. Transfer the tomato sauce into the bowl of the food processor or blender, and blend until smooth. Add salt and pepper to taste. Return the sauce to the saucepan, add the basil, and simmer an additional 15 minutes.

GRILLED SUMMER CORN AND TOMATILLO RELISH

YIELDS 6 TO 8 SERVINGS

I am so glad we have continually bred the corn plant to offer us the myriad of sweet nibbles that show up in our summer markets. I am very fond of the white kernel corn that is terrifically sweet. If I am not making a relish, soup, or what have you, I eat the corn raw. Three ears of corn and a green salad is one of the easiest dinners summer can offer me. If you are going to eat raw corn, make sure it is as fresh as possible, since the sugar in many varieties starts to convert to starch quickly.

4 ears of corn—as fresh as possible

½ pound fresh tomatillos

1 tablespoon toasted sesame oil

1 medium red onion—diced

1 chili pepper (very hot: serrano, habanero, or jalapeño)—seeds and membrane discarded, diced

2 teaspoons coriander—ground

⅛ cup cider vinegar

¼ cup cilantro leaves—chopped

Salt and black pepper to taste

Clean the corn of its husk and silky hairs. On a very hot grill cook the corn until it blisters and becomes lightly charred. Carefully cut the corn kernels from the cob.

Peel the husks from the tomatillos, wash, pat dry, and roughly chop.

Heat a 4-quart saucepan over a medium heat and add the oil. Add the onion and chili, cooking until the onions become translucent, about 5 minutes. Add the coriander and cook for 30 seconds longer. Add the tomatillos, corn, and cider vinegar. Reduce the heat to low and simmer covered for 15 minutes. Mix in the cilantro and season with salt and pepper. Serve warm or cold over grilled chicken, poached fish, or even try it as a side dish.

CORN AND CLAM CHOWDER
YIELDS 8 TO 10 SERVINGS

Summer is such a cold-food time of year and definitely not a friendly time for long-simmering pots. Yet chowders are absolute summer favorites, and fortunately they do not cook for extremely long periods of time. If you have a large enough barbecue, it can act as your outdoor stove top.

6 ears of corn—husked, silk removed, and cleaned

2 tablespoons olive oil

2 medium Vidalia onions—diced

4 stalks celery—diced

2 serrano chilies—seeds removed and diced

$\frac{1}{2}$ pound Yukon Gold potatoes—peeled and diced

3 garlic cloves—minced

$\frac{1}{2}$ cup white wine

2 quarts water

3 ripe tomatoes—seeds discarded and diced

$\frac{1}{2}$ pound fava beans

$\frac{1}{2}$ cup sage leaves—chopped

1 pound sugar snap peas—cut in half

$\frac{1}{2}$ pound zucchini—diced

1 tablespoon red wine vinegar

Salt and black pepper to taste

1 pound clams—washed to remove any sand from the shells

Cut corn kernels from their cobs and reserve both in separate bowls.

Heat an 8-quart soup pot over a medium flame and add the oil, onions, celery, and chilies, cooking until the onions lose their raw look, about 3 minutes. Add the potatoes, garlic, and white wine and cook until the wine has reduced to a glaze, about 4 minutes. Add the water, along with the corn cobs (not the kernels), diced tomatoes, fava beans, and half of the sage leaves. Bring to a boil and then reduce the flame, simmering for 30 to 45 minutes. At this point, remove the corn cobs from the chowder base and discard. Mix in the corn kernels, sugar snap peas, zucchini, the remaining sage leaves, vinegar, and salt and pepper. Bring the mixture back to a simmer and cook an additional 15 minutes. Add the clams and cover the pot and cook for 5 to 10 minutes.

Correct seasoning, if necessary, and serve with a wedge of lime and a dollop of sour cream.

CREAMED CORN SOUP

YIELDS 8 TO 10 SERVINGS

Notes

Adding mushrooms that have been sautéed to very crisp is a delightful variation on this soup.

I was watching the Food Channel one day and saw a chef puréeing fresh corn to use as a thickening agent for a sauce. The idea intrigued me. It was the height of the summer, and fresh, beautiful corn was in every market. I loved creamed corn as a kid (it came only canned), and memories of those sweet, soft mouthfuls came flooding back. Since I have recently returned from Mexico, where I sipped a wondrous cold cream of corn soup, this dairy-free summer soup took form.

10 ears of corn—husked, silk removed, and cleaned

2 medium yellow onions—thinly sliced

2 garlic cloves—roughly chopped

2 quarts vegetable stock

2 pablano peppers—whole

2 jalapeño peppers—whole

⅛ cup Texas tarragon (or a mix of cilantro and tarragon)

1 lime—juice only

Salt and black pepper to taste

Remove the kernels of corn from their cobs and set aside.

Place the cobs, onion, and garlic into a 6-quart soup pot along with the vegetable stock. Bring to a boil and simmer for 30 minutes, covered.

While the stock is simmering, take half of the corn kernels and purée in the food processor until it is completely smooth. Set aside.

Roast the pablano and jalapeño peppers in a hot skillet (preferably cast iron), turning them frequently to blister completely. Allow the peppers to cool slightly in a covered bowl and then remove the skin and seeds. Finely dice the peppers.

After the stock has finished simmering, remove the corn cobs and discard. In a food processor or blender, purée the stock to break down the garlic and onion. Return the soup to the pot along with the reserved puréed corn, remaining corn kernels, diced peppers, and tarragon. Bring to a boil and reduce the flame to a simmer. Gently simmer the soup for 15 minutes being careful not to let the soup scorch on the bottom. Season the soup with the lime juice, salt and pepper and serve hot or cold.

CHILLED CUCUMBER MINT SOUP

YIELDS 6 TO 8 SERVING

This soup is an homage to a Persian friend of mine who fed me numerous yogurt dishes and led me to a slew of ideas about food. In the sizzling heat of summer, a bowl full of this cooling concoction hits just the right spot. Try it with dill, oregano, or basil instead of the mint.

2 hothouse cucumbers—peeled and seeded

2 tablespoons salt

2 garlic cloves—crushed to a paste

2 tablespoons mint—leaves only, roughly chopped

2½ cups plain yogurt

1½ cups cold water

Black pepper and salt to taste

1 lemon, juice only

Shred the cucumber on the large holes of a cheese grater. Sprinkle the cucumber with the salt and let sit for 20 minutes in a colander to remove the excess liquid. Rinse the cucumber well under cold running water to rid it of any excess saltiness and drain.

Combine the cucumber, garlic, mint, and yogurt. Thin with the water and season with pepper and salt, if needed. Refrigerate for 1 hour or overnight. Squeeze a little lemon juice in each bowl just prior to serving.

YELLOW GAZPACHO

YIELDS 8 TO 10 SERVINGS

I adore this cold Spanish-inspired soup, and so does my mother. I have diced the vegetables every summer for as long as I remember to satisfy our summertime craving. Boredom did start to set in at a certain point—along with my undying need to change things. Then lo and behold a brave new world of tomatoes starting showing up in the market. I have made this soup using green zebra-striped tomatoes, various heirloom varieties, and even the sweet, succulent grape tomato (though be warned the latter are laborious). Now, during the heyday of summer, I do versions with all kinds of tomatoes, though the low-acidic nature of the yellow ones I favor the most.

6 yellow beefsteak tomatoes (approximately 1¾ pounds)

4 ribs celery—diced

6 scallions—diced

1 large cucumber—cut in half lengthwise, seeds removed, and diced

1 medium red onion—finely diced

½ cup cilantro leaves—roughly chopped

1 to 3 serrano peppers—seeds discarded and finely diced

1 lime—juiced (about ¼ cup)

1 jalapeño pepper—seeds discarded and finely diced

2 garlic cloves—crushed to a paste

2 tablespoons sherry or raspberry vinegar

¼ cup extra virgin olive oil

Salt and black pepper to taste

Tabasco sauce to taste

Plain yogurt or sour cream, to garnish

Cut the tomatoes in half through the circumference to expose the seed pocket. Gently squeeze the seeds and pulp in a strainer. Push down on the seeds and pulp catching the juice in a large bowl. Discard the seeds. Dice the remaining tomato meat and add the remaining ingredients into the strained tomato juice, except the salt and pepper and Tabasco sauce. Taste and correct seasoning with salt and pepper as well as additional lime juice or a shot or two of Tabasco sauce. Serve ice-cold with a dollop of plain yogurt or sour cream.

This soup has about a 2-day shelf life.

Love set before us
Taking on its daily form
Kisses for the cook

GNOCCHI WITH CHERRY TOMATOES AND SAGE BUTTER

YIELDS 8 TO 10 SERVINGS

My knack for gnocchi comes from my dear friend's mother, who is Croatian. She taught me that the potato dough should be moist but not too wet, the gentle touch needed to roll out the log shape, and then, the final forming of the gnocchi. The only real changes I made to her splendid puffs of potato dough are using oil in lieu of butter and the bit of nutmeg, but I don't think Angela would mind. The addition of the cherry tomatoes brightens this classic dish with one of summer's moments.

> 3 russet potatoes (approximately 1½ pounds)
>
> 2 cups all-purpose flour (plus additional flour for dusting)
>
> 3 large eggs
>
> ¼ cup olive oil
>
> 1 teaspoon nutmeg
>
> 2 tablespoons salt

Bring a 2-quart pot of water to a boil and cook the potatoes in their jackets until they are fork-tender, about 15 to 20 minutes. Remove from the heat and allow to cool slightly. Then peel the skin off and put the potatoes through a potato ricer. On a clean, lightly floured work surface place the potatoes and make a large well in the middle. Sprinkle about 1¼ cups of the flour over the potatoes. Add the eggs, olive oil, nutmeg, and salt into the well and mix to combine. Start mixing the combined potato/flour into the egg mixture and work to combine it all together. If the gnocchi mixture feels wet and tacky, work in additional flour.

On a floured work surface, divide the potato dough into 6 pieces. Roll each piece into a log approximately 1-inch round by about 12-inches long. Cut the log into ½-inch pieces. You can either lightly pinch the gnocchi or you may lightly roll the piece up the back of a fork to create some ridges. Place the prepared gnocchi on a clean, well-floured kitchen towel to help prevent it from sticking to a tray.

Cherry Tomato and Sage Butter

¾ pound unsalted butter

¼ cup sage leaves—shredded

2 pints cherry tomatoes cut in half (if they are much larger than the gnocchi)

Place the butter and sage in a saucepan over a medium-low heat. Simmer the butter until it turns golden brown, being careful not to burn it. Add the cherry tomatoes and remove from the heat. Keep warm until ready to use.

Gently drop the gnocchi into a 6- or 8-quart pot of boiling water and cook until they float to the surface, approximately 4 minutes. Drain the gnocchi and divide among individual plates or a large platter and spoon over the Cherry Tomato and Sage Butter. Serve immediately, garnished with a sage leaf. You may also freeze the gnocchi.

GRILLED EGGPLANT AND WHIPPED FETA TORTA

YIELDS 6 SERVINGS

Yummm . . . The whipped feta and potatoes are fantastic alone with just pita bread chips and a bowl of olives as hors d'oeuvres. Piled on, the eggplant dresses it up to create an elegant first course. These tortas can be assembled up to 1 day in advance, covered, and refrigerated, leaving no last-minute hassles.

> 3 medium-sized eggplant—cut into ½-inch rounds
>
> ½ pound russet potatoes (approximately 1 large potato)
>
> 2 garlic cloves—crushed to a paste
>
> 2 lemons—zest and juice
>
> ½ cup olive oil
>
> 1 pound feta cheese
>
> Salt and pepper to taste
>
> 2 red peppers—diced, to garnish

Preheat the oven to 350°F.

On a very hot grill, cook the eggplant rounds to mark them nicely, and then transfer them to a baking tray. Brush the rounds with olive oil and finish cooking in the oven until tender. This prevents the eggplant from getting too charred on the grill. Let the eggplant cool to room temperature. If you don't have a grill, cook the eggplant for about 10 minutes in the oven at 400°F.

Peel the potato and cook in boiling water until fork-tender about 15 to 20 minutes. Place the potato on a tray and bake for 5 minutes to let any excess moisture evaporate. Mash the potato until smooth and set aside.

Place the garlic, lemon zest and juice, olive oil, feta, and salt and pepper in a food processor and blend until creamy. Add the potato and mix by hand to thoroughly incorporate. Correct seasoning, if needed.

To assemble, place a slice of eggplant on a plate and place a heaping tablespoon of the potato/feta mixture on top. Then place another eggplant on top of the potato/feta mixture, and another heaping tablespoon of the potato/feta mixture. Place a third eggplant on of this one. Pour about 1 ounce of Basil/Oregano Oil over the torta and garnish with diced red peppers.

Basil/Oregano Oil

> **2 cups basil—leaves only**
>
> **1 cup oregano—leaves only**
>
> **2 garlic cloves—minced**
>
> **¼ cup ground almonds**
>
> **Salt and pepper**
>
> **2 cups olive oil**

Place the herbs, garlic, almonds, salt and pepper in a blender or food processor. Process to break down the herbs and have everything roughly chopped. With the motor running, drizzle in the oil. This makes about 2 cups.

Notes
This oil is also wonderful tossed into pasta, or brushed on to fish prior to grilling or baking. You can even thin it out with some white wine vinegar for a salad dressing.

GRILLED CHICKEN BREASTS WITH SUMMER SQUASH

YIELDS 6 SERVINGS

This is a great low-maintenance dish that allows you to lift chicken breast out of the pan along with its accompanying vegetables. If you can't find the small pattypan squash (also known as sunburst squash) use a small zucchini instead. You don't have to pregrill the chicken for this recipe. I would simply bake the chicken and vegetables and for the last few minutes, pass it under the broiler to brown the chicken breasts.

6 chicken breasts—halved, skinned, and boned

1 lemon—juiced

Salt and freshly ground black pepper to taste

⅓ cup olive oil

4 plum tomatoes—quartered

24 Kalamata olives—pitted

½ cup capers—drained

24 pattypan squash

2 large red peppers—roasted, skinned, and seeded, cut into ½-inch thick strips

1 cup Lemon/Mustard Dressing

Preheat an outdoor grill or stovetop grill pan to very hot.

Toss the chicken with the lemon juice, salt and pepper, and olive oil to coat. Place on the hot grill, and cook about 5 minutes. You want to get a good "scoring"—that is, grill marks—on the meat.

Preheat the oven to 375°F.

Mix the tomatoes, olives, capers, squash, and red peppers together, and place in the bottom of an ovenproof 12 x 9 inch pan. Lay the chicken over the vegetables. Pour on the Lemon/Mustard Dressing and cook for about 15 minutes in the oven. To serve, lift a chicken breast out of the pan along with the vegetables bedded underneath. Spoon over some of the Lemon/Mustard Dressing. This dish is wonderful over your favorite pasta or Green Rice (page 99).

Lemon/Mustard Dressing

   2 lemons—juice only

   2 tablespoons balsamic vinegar

   4 tablespoons Dijon mustard

   Salt and white pepper to taste

   ¾ cup extra virgin olive oil

Combine the lemon juice, balsamic vinegar, mustard, salt and pepper together, and then slowly whisk in the oil.

CHICKEN FILLET WITH ROASTED PEPPERS, ROSEMARY, AND CHILI

YIELDS 4 SERVINGS

Notes

This tasty dish can be served as a main course, tossed with your favorite pasta, or served over crusty peasant bread as a first course.

This is a dish I learned to make while living in Australia, but its Italian flavor gives away the heritage of the chef who gave me the recipe. The small Asian chilies used here have a good incendiary quality. However, if jalapeños are all you can find, they will do. I just tend to double the amount. I like it hot!

1 pound chicken breasts—boned and skinned

1 tablespoon olive oil

2 red asian chilies—seeds discarded and diced

4 red peppers—roasted and sliced into ¼-inch strips

¼ cup balsamic vinegar

4⅛ cup rosemary—leaves only, roughly chopped

5 stalks scallions—sliced on an angle

Salt and freshly ground black pepper to taste

Cut the chicken breasts into thirds. In an 10-inch sauté pan, heat the oil to hot. Add the chicken and chilies, and sauté until the chicken is golden brown, about 3 minutes on each side. Add the red peppers and toss to incorporate with the chicken. Continue cooking until the chicken is done (approximately 10 minutes), and immediately add the balsamic vinegar, rosemary, and scallions. Season with salt and black pepper and serve.

SALMON FILLETS MARINATED IN MINT AND LEMON

This is such a versatile recipe for which you can use different herbs such as tarragon, basil, rosemary, or thyme—it is their stems that are being used here to give flavor. Or use tuna or skewered shrimp and scallops as your fish. I always enjoy the flavor imparted by the grill on a piece of fish, but if a grill is not available to you, roast the fish in a 375°F oven for 10 minutes.

12 mint stems—chopped

½ lemon—sliced into thin rounds

6 4-ounce salmon fillets

½ lemon—juiced

¼ cup vodka

Salt and freshly ground black pepper to taste

In an 8 x 8 glass baking dish, lay down half of the mint and lemon slices. Put the salmon fillets on top, and then place remaining mint and lemon over the salmon fillets. Combine the lemon juice and vodka, and then pour over the salmon. Refrigerate for 1 to 2 hours.

Preheat the grill to very hot, or preheat the oven to 375°F.

Prior to cooking the fish, remove the lemon and mint and season with salt and pepper. Cook the fish for 10 minutes. If grilling the fillets, you will want to turn the fish 3 to 4 times in order to prevent it from getting too charred. Serve immediately with Strawberry Tomato Salsa (page 63) or Grilled Summer Corn and Tomatillo Relish (page 67).

GRILLED SQUID

YIELDS 6 SERVINGS

The young garlic tops found in this recipe are the tender stalks and unopened flower heads of the extremely odiferous bulb. They are, of course, a note of more pungent moments to come, but at this point in their growth, their aroma is gentle enough to be relished raw. Use them to finish a summer tomato sauce or toss with grilled chicken and pasta. If garlic tops are unavailable to you, try garlic chives, or simply very thinly sliced garlic cloves.

> **2 pounds squid—cleaned**
>
> **Salt and black pepper to taste**
>
> **⅛ pound garlic green tops**
>
> **½ cup sorrel leaves—roughly chopped**
>
> **¼ cup extra virgin olive oil**

Heat an indoor grill pan or outdoor grill to very hot.

Make sure the squid is dried of any excessive moisture, and season lightly with salt and pepper. Quickly grill the garlic tops for about 3 minutes, turning a couple of times to prevent them from burning. Grill the squid for 4 to 5 minutes, turning once. Toss the squid, garlic tops, and remaining ingredients together and serve warm.

POACHED LOBSTER TAILS

YIELDS 6 SERVINGS

When I was growing up on the northeastern shores of the Atlantic, lobsters were a constant summertime meal along with local blue claw crabs and steamers. I harbor warm thoughts and vivid memories of our entire neighborhood turning out to share in the bounty of our local waters. Today, wearing my chef's toque, I'm more apt to prepare lobster grilled or even smoked. This recipe gives my palate the finesse required to excite it, with the ease of boiling. The hyssop offers a subtle anise perfume to this dish that is ideal with a nicely chilled glass of Sauvignon Blanc or an Alsacean Gewürtztraminer.

- 2 cups water
- 2 cups white wine
- 10 stems hyssop (or fennel leaves)
- 6 lobster tails

In a high-sided 12-inch sauté pan that will accommodate the lobster tails in a single layer, place the water, wine, and hyssop stems. Bring the mixture to a simmer and add the lobster tails. Cook the lobster for 12 to 14 minutes. Remove from the poaching liquid and let cool. Split the bottom side of the lobster tails to expose its meat with a pair of kitchen scissors and gently loosen the lobster from its shell. (You may want to trim away the bottom side of the lobster with the kitchen scissors altogether, as a presentation element.)

Dressing

- ⅛ cup hyssop leaves (or ¼ cup chopped fennel bulb)
- ¼ champagne vinegar
- 1 tablespoon Dijon mustard
- ¾ cup olive oil
- Salt and pepper to taste

To make the dressing, place all of the ingredients in a blender and purée until smooth.

Correct seasoning and use as either a dipping sauce or pour over the lobster meat resting on a bed of baby salad greens.

STEAMED FILLET OF FISH

YIELDS 4 SERVINGS

The town of Bukittinggi on the island of Sumatra is situated just off the equator, high in the mountains. The market here is laden with the bounty of the island—deep rich chilies, bushes of feathery cilantro, extra-long snake beans, three-foot-tall lemon grass, as well as beautifully displayed garlands of flowers waiting to adorn a family's altar. In this market are eating establishments called *Warungs.* They are basically tented wok stands with some tables around them. Here I dined on a luscious steam whole fish scented ever so delicately with lemon grass and chilies.

> 2 stalks lemon grass—top quarter discarded
>
> 2 to 3 Asian red chilies—pierced with a knife
>
> ½ cup cilantro stem and root—washed and chopped
>
> ½-inch piece of ginger root—sliced
>
> Olive oil
>
> 4 6-ounce fish fillets—such as sole, orange roughy, or flounder

Slice the lemon grass into thin pieces. Place the lemon grass, chilies, cilantro, and ginger root in a wide 6-quart saucepan or wok and cover with 2 inches of water. Bring to a boil and cover. Reduce the heat to low and gently simmer for 10 minutes to infuse the flavors into the water. If using a saucepan, place two teacups on the bottom in order to balance a steaming tray on it. For a wok, you can use either a bamboo steaming tray or a rack that fits the width of the wok. Lightly oil the steaming tray (this helps prevent the fish from sticking), and lay the fish down. Lower into the steamer, and cook with a tight-fitting lid for 10 minutes. It is important that the fish does not come in direct contact with the water.

Serve immediately with Cilantro-Mint Pesto (page 65).

MARINATED GRILLED SWORDFISH

YIELDS 6 SERVINGS

Walking through Palermo, Sicily, I came across a series of backstreets that served as a central market for the city. The smell of cooling focaccia intermingling with different cheeses and other potent aromas was fanned by the strongly blowing sirocco winds. The sight of swordfish now immediately transports me back to that market, right in front of the fishmonger's stall. Thai mint is a curiously strong basil/mint flavor that has smallish pointed leaves.

2 stalks lemon grass

½ cup Thai mint—leaves only (or a combination of mint and basil)

1 red Asian chili—seeds removed and diced (or any hot chili pepper such as serrano or habanero)

1-inch long piece of ginger root—peeled and finely diced

6 swordfish fillets (weighing approximately 5 ounces each)

Salt and black pepper to taste

⅛ cup toasted sesame oil

Trim the lemon grass at its base and then trim off the green top portion. Discard the lemon grass where the green top starts to fade into the white bottom. Finely chop the lemon grass and Thai mint, and combine with the chili and ginger. Rub the mixture into the swordfish fillets, and wrap each individually in plastic wrap. If you use your hands to spread the marinade onto the swordfish, I strongly recommend you wear plastic gloves.

Refrigerate for 8 hours—or up to 24 hours.

Preheat an indoor stove grill or outdoor grill.

Remove the plastic wrap and season with salt and pepper. Cook over a very hot grill for about 10 minutes. Drizzle the sesame oil over the fillets as they come off the grill. Serve immediately with Sautéed Chayote Squash (page 106).

SAUSAGE GUMBO

YIELDS 6 TO 8 SERVINGS

The name gumbo itself is derived from an African word for okra. In this stew you can use whatever sausage you like best—I am very partial to an Andouille-style smoked pheasant sausage that I find in New York City's Union Square market. Play with different sausages and feel free to try new vegetables as well. Filé powder is a thickening agent made from the ground dried leaves of the sassafras tree, which has a strong herbaceous scent, but if used in a small enough amount, it won't overwhelm the dish. Outside the southern part of the United States, it can be found in gourmet shops or ordered through spice merchants such as Penzeys.

1½ pound smoked sausage

3 small white eggplant (or globe eggplant)

¼ pound burdock root (or salisfy)

¼ pound snake squash (or zucchini)

2 tablespoons olive oil

1 large onion—diced

3 cloves garlic—chopped

1 pound okra—trimmed and cut in half

1 cup red wine

2 cups tomato purée (this can be canned or freshly puréed tomatoes with seeds removed)

½ cup water

¼ cup summer savory—leaves only, roughly chopped

Salt and black pepper to taste

1 teaspoon filé powder

Heat a grill to very hot and score the sausage with good grill marks. This charring will help add a nice density to the finished gumbo. Slice the sausage into 1-inch rounds and reserve to the side.

Dice the eggplant into 1-inch squares and set aside.

Peel the burdock root and cut into ½-inch rounds. Make sure you have a bowl of tap water by your work area to place the sliced burdock root, since it oxides very quickly. Leave the burdock in the water until ready to use.

Slice the snake squash into ½-inch rounds.

Heat a heavily lined 6-quart stew pot over a high heat and add the oil and diced onion. Sauté until the onion is lightly browned, about 10 minutes, and then add the eggplant, burdock, and garlic. Continue to cook for 5 minutes, stirring occasionally. Next mix in the snake squash, okra, sausage, and red wine. Bring the mixture to a boil and reduce the liquid by half. This will take about 5–7 minutes. Pour in the tomato purée, the water, and half of the summer savory. Reduce the heat to low and simmer the gumbo for 30 minutes. Season with salt and pepper and add the remaining summer savory. Mix in the filé powder and shut off the heat. Filé powder has a tendency to go stringy if boiled. Serve immediately.

ON THE SIDE

GRILLED SUMMER CORN AND SUGAR SNAP PEA SALAD

YIELDS APPROXIMATELY 6 TO 8 SERVINGS

Buying a bag of sugar snap peas for me is like walking home with a fresh loaf of bread—I need a spare. I cannot resist crunching away on those sugary, tender green pods. Once home, they need the slightest wave over a flame and they are ready to be presented. Purchase sugar snap peas that are full, dark green, and crisp; and use them as soon as possible, since their flavor starts to fade as soon as they are harvested. To prepare, just snap the stem tip and gently pull toward the other end to remove the fibrous membrane that runs down the center of the pea.

> 4 ears of corn—as fresh as possible
>
> 1 tablespoon olive oil
>
> 1 small red onion—diced
>
> 1 chili pepper (very hot)—diced (such as serrano, habanero or jalapeño)
>
> 2 teaspoons cumin seed—ground
>
> 1/2 pound sugar snap peas—cut in thirds
>
> 1/8 cup red wine vinegar
>
> 1/4 cup Italian parsley leaves—chopped
>
> Salt and black pepper to taste

Peel the husks from the corn and remove the silk. On a very hot grill, cook the corn to blister and lightly char. Carefully cut the corn kernels from the cob.

Heat a 2-quart saucepan over a medium heat and add the olive oil. Add the onion and chili pepper, cooking until the onions become translucent, about 3–5 minutes. Add the cumin and cook for 30 seconds. Add the sugar snap peas and cook for about 3 minutes to "off" the rawness of the peas. Remove from the heat, mix in the corn, the red wine vinegar, and parsley, then season with salt and pepper. Serve warm or cold.

Serve this dish with a meal of Salmon Marinated in Lemon and Mint (page 83) and Roasted Potato Salad (page 93).

HUSK TOMATO AND CORN SALAD

YIELDS 6 TO 8 SERVINGS

Notes

Try drying the husk tomatoes—lay them on a screen or fine-mesh strainer and place them in a cool dry spot. If they are not in a single layer, give them a toss once a day to help prevent them for getting moldy. Let them sit for about 1 week. Eat them as a snack, or freeze them and put them in your Thanksgiving Cranberry Relish. If husk tomatoes are not available in your area, try golden raspberries or gooseberries in this recipe.

The husk tomato, along with its close relative the tomatillo, are not tomatoes at all, but rather, distant cousins of the tomato. All these plants are indigenous to the North America and are being found more readily as we rediscover our culinary heritage. The husk tomato has a lanternlike husk with a large pea-size fruit that is pale yellow when ripe. The flavor of the fruit is a musky-pineapple that marries well to both savory and sweet applications. Be warned, they are addictive!

4 ears of white corn

1 pint husk tomatoes

1 hot chili pepper—such as a habenero

2 limes—juiced

1 tablespoon toasted sesame oil

¼ pound snow pea sprouts

Salt and black pepper to taste

Cut the corn kernels from their cob and place in a bowl.

Peel the husks from the tomatoes and wash.

Split the chili in half and remove the seeds.

Finely dice the chili.

Toss all the ingredients together. Let the salad sit for 30 minutes at room temperature before serving to let the flavors meld.

ROASTED POTATO SALAD

YIELDS 6 SERVINGS

I am so attracted to the first earth-encrusted potatoes of the season, and I am so pleased with the growing number of varieties now available. It amuses me to see all these new potatoes with names that hearken back to some ancient European lineage like "French Fingerling" and "Russian Banana." In fact the potato is believed to originate in the Andes Mountains of Ecuador and Peru and was not introduced to Europe until sometime in the sixteenth century. Head to a Latin market and encounter a whole new world of potatoes.

1½ **pounds small new potatoes (such as red bliss; Yukon Gold, or purple Peruvian)**

½ **cup olive oil**

1 medium Vidalia onion—sliced thinly

1 pint cherry tomatoes

⅛ **cup Mexican mint (or a mix of cilantro and tarragon)—chopped**

¼ **cup red wine vinegar**

Salt and black pepper to taste

Preheat the oven to 375°F.

Wash and dry the potatoes, then toss with the olive oil. Lay the potatoes on a baking tray in a single layer. Place in the oven and roast until tender and crisped, approximately 15 to 20 minutes. With 5 minutes remaining in the cooking, sprinkle the onion over the potatoes and let them wilt.

In a large bowl place the tomatoes, Mexican mint, vinegar, and the hot potatoes and onions. Gently toss and season with salt and pepper. Let the mixture cool and serve at room temperature or cold. This is a great picnic item.

RED AND YELLOW MARBLE SALAD

YIELDS 8 SERVINGS

Notes

The type of chili and herbs are of less importance here and I encourage you to let your palate be your guide. However, try to maintain the color play of the potatoes and the small cherry tomatoes.

When the twelve varieties of apples have dwindle to one or two, and sweet potatoes are nowhere to be found, I know the season is upon me. It is late June, and the first new potatoes have arrived. Not the golf-ball-size ones we are all used to and love, but rather, tiny marble-size beauties. I excitedly dig through baskets filled to the brim to get to these starchy gems, which always seem to end up on the bottom—Yukon golds, red bliss, purple Peruvians—none are safe from my probing hands.

¼ pound baby red potatoes

¼ pound Baby Yukon Gold potatoes

½ cup extra virgin olive oil

1 pint red cherry tomatoes—halved

1 pint yellow cherry tomatoes—halved

1 green chili—diced (such as jalapeño or serrano)

⅛ cup champagne vinegar or white wine vinegar

1 lime—zested and juiced

1 cup tightly packed arugula leaves—roughly chopped

Salt and black pepper to taste

Preheat the oven to 375°F.

Toss the potatoes with the oil and place on a baking tray. Cook the potatoes in the oven for 20 to 25 minutes until tender and slightly blistered.

With the potatoes still warm, gently toss together with all the remaining ingredients in a bowl. Refrigerate 2 hours before serving.

CUCUMBER AND MINT SALAD

YIELDS 6 TO 8 SERVINGS

When I was a child, there was always a large jar of pickling cucumbers in the refrigerator all summer long. My poor mother had a difficult time keeping up with the demand—everyone was constantly sneaking into the jar. I can still hear her exasperated cry: "They're not ready yet!"

2 large cucumbers—peeled and halved lengthwise

3 tablespoons salt

1 large white onion—sliced thin

½ cup mint leaves—chopped

2 teaspoons white pepper

1 cup white wine vinegar

Scoop out the seed pulp of the cucumber, and slice into ¼-inch half-moon pieces. Toss the cucumber with the salt and place in a colander. Let sit for 30 minutes, and then wash under cold running water. Pat the cucumber slices dry.

In a large bowl toss the cucumbers, onion, mint, and pepper to thoroughly combine. Place the cucumber mixture into a 2-quart glass, porcelain, or earthenware jar with a nonmetallic lid. Add the vinegar and shake well to distribute the flavors. Refrigerate for minimum of 24 hours. This salad will keep for 2 weeks in the refrigerator.

CHOPPED SALAD

YIELDS 6 TO 8

I can make a meal of a salad, and this one is always a comfort for me. Part of what I adore about this salad is that is will last a few days in the refrigerator. Although the spinach will wilt, it doesn't get "slimy" like more tender leafy greens do as they sit. Change the vegetable in this salad as you see fit, using broccoli, jicama, or chayote squash as they come into season.

¼ pound pancetta (an unsmoked Italian bacon)

1 tablespoon canola oil

1 ear of corn—husk and silk removed

1 large red pepper—seeds and membrane removed

1 small red onion

¼ cup Kalamata olives—pitted

1 bunch spinach (approx. 4 tightly packed cups)—washed thoroughly and dried

1 cup cherry tomatoes—halved

½ cup basil leaves—torn

2 cups cauliflower florets

Slice the pancetta into ½-inch long strips. Heat an 8-inch sauté pan to hot and add the canola oil along with the pancetta. Cook the pancetta to crispy, drain on paper towels, and reserve.

Cut the kernels off the corn. The corn is eaten raw, so it should be as farm-fresh as possible. Dice the red pepper and red onion into ½-inch squares. Roughly chop the olives and spinach. Add the cherry tomatoes and basil.

Blanch the cauliflower in boiling water for 3 to 4 minutes. They should still have a nice crunch. Refresh under cold water to stop the cooking process. Drain.

Toss all the ingredients together along with approximately 1 cup of Italian dressing.

Italian Dressing

¼ cup white wine vinegar

2 tablespoons basil—leaves only, chopped

2 teaspoons thyme—leaves only, chopped

1 tablespoon oregano—leaves only, chopped

1 garlic clove—crushed to a paste

Salt and black pepper to taste

1 cup olive oil

Mix all ingredients together, except the oil. In a slow stream, whisk in the oil until all is incorporated. This makes about 1½ cups.

ICED RADISHES

YIELDS 6 SERVINGS

This is one of those recipes that so clearly proves nature does it best. It is simple yet absolutely delicious. I have always relished the crunch and peppery bitterness of these little tubers, but after a meal in a Vietnamese restaurant where I had fried squid with a pepper-lemon dipping sauce, an idea arose. The sourness of the lemon helps mellow the back-of-the-throat palate that usually accompanies each bite.

> 2 bunches red or white icicle radishes
>
> 3 lemons—juiced
>
> 2 tablespoons salt
>
> 2 teaspoons black pepper

Wash the radishes and trim off the greens.

Toss the radishes, lemon juice, salt, and pepper together in a ceramic, stainless steel, or glass bowl to thoroughly combine. Chill in the refrigerator for 30 minutes and serve very cold. Serve as part of a summer antipasto platter.

GREEN RICE
YIELDS 6 SERVINGS

I am a rice fanatic and enjoy a simple bowl of plain cooked rice. This rice dish, however, gives me everything I love . . . a gentle grain, great bold flavor, and a lightly crisp bottom. Yes, the rice dish, if done well, has a fabulous crisp, bottomed crust. This rice reminds me of a style of Persian rice cooking called "tah dig," which means crisp bottom.

1½ cup long grain rice

4 cups hot water

1 cup vegetable or chicken stock

1 garlic clove—roughly chopped

1 cup Italian parsley—leaves only

½ cup cilantro—leaves only

⅛ cup mint—leaves only

1 tablespoon salt

2 teaspoons freshly ground black pepper

⅓ cup vegetable oil

1 small onion—finely diced

2 pablano chilies—roasted, peeled, and seeded, and cut into thin strips

Put the rice into a bowl and pour the very hot tap water over to cover; stir and let sit for 20 minutes. Drain and rinse under cold water for about 3 minutes.

Place the stock, the garlic, parsley, cilantro, mint, salt, and pepper in the blender and process until puréed. Set aside.

Heat a 1-quart saucepan over a medium-high heat and add the oil. Then add the rice and fry for 5 minutes. Be sure to keep it moving so as not to burn it. Add the onion and pablano chilies and continue cooking for about 3 minutes longer. Add the herb purée to the rice and reduce the heat to very low. Cover the pot with a dampened cloth towel, then place the lid on top, and continue cooking for 25 minutes. Remove from the heat and let sit 15 minutes before serving.

MINTED BULGAR

YIELDS 6 SERVINGS

Notes
This dish can be served hot or cold. To warm, place in an oven-safe dish and heat in a 175°F oven.

This recipe calls for vegetable stock, which should be homemade. Canned vegetable stock is going to have an enormous amount of salt added to it. It's so easy to make yourself. Simply rough-chop a couple of onions, carrots, celery ribs, garlic cloves, parsley stems, and a bay leaf and place them in an 8-quart pot. Pour water over the vegetables, coming up about 4 inches above the vegetables. Bring to a boil and simmer for 45 minutes. Strain and there you have it. Freeze all leftover stock in 1-quart- and 1/2-quart-size containers for up to 3 months. You could also add fennel, celery root, parsnips, turnips, and mushrooms to the stock. I also use the trimmings of some vegetables, since there is great flavor trapped in these inedible parts.

2½ cups vegetable stock or water

1 cup bulgar wheat

1 pint cherry tomatoes—halved

6 scallions—diced

4 stalks celery—diced

¼ cup Italian parsley leaves—chopped

½ bunch mint leaves—chopped

⅛ cup low-sodium soy sauce

White pepper to taste

In a 1-quart saucepan, bring the stock to a boil, and pour in the bulgar. Bring it back to a boil, and then lower to a simmer and cover. Cook for approximately 25 minutes. Let the bulgar stand covered for 10 minutes off the heat. Fluff the bulgar with a fork, and cool completely. Toss in the remaining ingredients.

BAKED TURNIPS

YIELDS 4 SERVINGS

I was so used to buying turnip, collard, and mustard greens separately, and always enjoyed eating them in various ways. Then, when small baby turnips started showing up in the market with their leaves still attached, I thought, what a bonus . . . two meals in one! Eventually this turned into a do-it-all-at-once cooking moment. Try this technique with baby beets as well.

12 small turnips with leaves still attached

¼ cup olive oil

Salt and black pepper to taste

Preheat the oven to 350°F.

Wash and trim the root base from the turnips. Discard any leaves that look sorely worn.

Line a roasting pan with aluminum foil, covering its edges. Lay the turnips down, with the stem and leaves folded under the turnip bulb. Drizzle with olive oil and season with salt and pepper. Tightly cover the turnips with more aluminum foil, and bake for 30 minutes. Serve immediately to complete any dish.

SAUTÉED PEAS AND FENNEL

YIELDS 8 SERVINGS

My mother hates when I say this, but I did not experience a fresh pea until I was in my late teens. Prior to that I thought that peas always came with carrots . . . canned, and I absolutely despised them. What a revelation to encounter the sweet joy of this legume. I never allow them to overcook, and if I am using them in a soup, stew, or risotto, I add them during the last 10 minutes.

> 3 cups fresh peas (approximately 2 pounds)
>
> 2 fennel bulbs—trimmed and diced
>
> ½ cup white wine
>
> ⅛ cup olive oil
>
> Salt and black pepper to taste

In a high-sided 8-inch sauté pan, add the peas, fennel bulbs, and white wine, and cook over medium flame for 10 minutes. Add the oil and salt and pepper to taste. Keep warm and serve.

Snuggling little peas
the season's cycle wins
To the earth . . . tumbling

STUFFED ZUCCHINI
YIELDS 6 SERVINGS

One of my best and most memorable holidays was staying with a group of friends in the south of France in a house where the biggest complaint was that the pool was too far from the back door. Every day I toured the surrounding postcard vistas and made daily visits to the local town markets. This recipe was inspired by one of those shopping jaunts. Although I have been able to replicate it here at home, I have not found almonds still clinging to theirs branches for me to use on a whim.

> 6 medium-sized pattypan squash or 3 small zucchini
>
> 5 ounces goat cheese
>
> ¼ cup Niçoise olives—pitted and chopped
>
> ¼ cup blanched almonds—chopped
>
> ½ cup chives—chopped
>
> 5 sprigs oregano—leaves only, chopped (approx. 2 tablespoons)
>
> Salt and black pepper to taste
>
> ⅛ cup olive oil

Preheat the oven to 350°F.

Cut the pattypan squash in half through its circumference. If using zucchini, cut in half lengthwise. Scoop out and reserve two-thirds of the pulp, being careful not to make a hole in the bottom of the squash halves. Set aside.

Chop the pulp and mix with the goat cheese, olives, almonds, chives, oregano, salt and pepper. Divide the mixture among the squash halves, and drizzle with the olive oil. Place on a tray, and bake for 10 to 15 minutes. Serve immediately.

MINT-SCENTED ZUCCHINI
YIELDS 6 SERVINGS

This recipe is an Italian-inspired dish where they marinate fried zucchini with mint and vinegar. It's truly wonderful. The addition of lightly toasted pine nuts and raisins would also work with this combination. I like to buy zucchini that are on the smaller side, since their seed pockets have not fully developed and the flavor is less bitter.

6 small zucchini

¼ cup olive oil

½ cup red wine vinegar

½ cup mint—leaves only

3 garlic cloves—finely chopped

Salt and black pepper to taste

Toasted pine nuts, as garnish

Raisins, as garnish

Slice the zucchini on an angle, ¼-inch thick. Spread out on a baking rack and let air-dry for 1 hour.

Heat a 10-inch sauté pan and add the olive oil. Carefully fry the zucchini, in small batches, until golden brown, about 3 to 4 minutes. Drain on paper towels.

Mix the red wine vinegar, mint, garlic, salt and pepper in a 2-cup saucepan. Warm over medium heat. Arrange the zucchini in a single layer on a platter, and then spoon the warm mint and vinegar mixture over the zucchini. If adding raisins and pine nuts, sprinkle them over the zucchini before pouring on the vinegar. Let the zucchini sit at room temperature for 1 hour or overnight in the refrigerator before serving.

SAUTÉED CHAYOTE SQUASH

YIELDS 6 SERVINGS

I have met this squash under so many different names: choko in Australia, mirliton in the Southeast, christophine in the Caribbean, and chayote on the West Coast. Whatever its name, this North American native is low maintenance and delicious. It has an edible pale green skin and seed as well as a meat that is crisp and cucumberlike. Eat it raw in salads, soups, sautés, or purées. It will last about 1 month in the refrigerator.

3 chayote squash

3 plum tomatoes—seeds discarded

2 tablespoons olive oil

1 medium onion—sliced thin

$\frac{1}{8}$ cup white wine vinegar

2 garlic cloves—diced

2 tablespoons thyme—chopped

1 tablespoon chives—chopped

Salt and freshly ground black pepper to taste

Peel the skin from the chayote and then cut in half from pole to pole to expose two halves of the seed. Remove and discard the seed. Slice the chayote into $\frac{1}{4}$-inch thick sticks. Slice the tomatoes to $\frac{1}{4}$-inch thick strips.

Heat an 8-inch sauté pan to hot, and add the oil and onion. Sauté the onions for 15 minutes or until golden brown over a medium-low flame.

Once the onions are golden, add the vinegar and garlic, and cook for about 3 minutes longer. Add the chayote, tomatoes, thyme, chives, salt and pepper and cook covered over a medium-low flame for 10 more minutes. Correct seasoning and serve immediately with fish, poultry, or meats.

Gathering nourish
comfort for body and soul
attended by all

DESSERTS

LEMON VERBENA SORBET

YIELDS APPROXIMATELY 1 QUART

I dream of having a garden. Standing sentinel at the entrance would be two healthy, bushy verbena plants frisking each visitor with their luscious, aromatic arms. In this sorbet you must use fresh verbena, as dried will not soften enough to allow a pleasant palate experience. These homemade sorbets have about a 2-week shelf life since, with the small portion of corn syrup in the recipe, the ice eventually starts to crystallize. On a hot summer evening there is no better treat, and may well be worth the investment in an ice-cream maker.

1 cup champagne

2 teaspoons fresh lemon juice

1 tablespoon lemon verbena leaves—finely minced

1 teaspoon light corn syrup

½ cup water

2 egg whites

½ cup superfine sugar

Mix the champagne, lemon juice, lemon verbena, light corn syrup, and water together.

In a clean, dry bowl, beat the egg whites to a soft peak, and then slowly sprinkle in the sugar. Continue beating the egg whites back to a stiff peak. Fold the egg whites into the champagne mixture and place into the freezing compartment of an ice-cream maker. Proceed according to the manufacturer's instructions.

YELLOW WATERMELON SORBET

Of course you can use a traditional watermelon here with just as fabulous results. The yellow watermelon is slightly more subtle in flavor and the mint brings in a bit of a kick. If orange-scented mint is not available to you, add 1 teaspoon of orange zest to the sorbet.

3 pounds yellow watermelon

¼ cup water

1 cup sugar

10 stems orange mint—leaves only, chopped (approx. ¼ cup)

Cut up the watermelon and remove the meat from the rind. Discard all the seeds. Purée the meat in a blender or food processor.

In a 2-cup saucepan, place the water and sugar, cover, and bring to a boil. Keeping the mixture covered helps prevent the sugar from crystallizing. Cook for 3 minutes covered and then remove the lid and continue cooking for an additional 3 minutes. Cool the sugar syrup completely.

In a bowl, mix the watermelon puree and sugar syrup together until well combined. Pour this into the freezing compartment of an ice-cream maker. Proceed according to the manufacturer's freezing instructions. Once the sorbet has formed and is very frosty, add the chopped mint to distribute it. Transfer the sorbet to a 2-quart freezer container and place in the freezer to completely set the sorbet. The sorbet will keep for about 1 week.

GOOSEBERRY, APRICOT, AND CHERRY COMPOTE

YIELDS 8 SERVINGS

Gooseberries are round, engorged orbs with a pale green coloration that offers a nice tangy palate. Married with the brilliant sweetness of the cherries and the more subtle tartness of apricots, you end up with a full-body compote. An interesting twist would be to remove the sugar from the recipe and cook the fruit with a splash of white wine vinegar, some cracked black pepper, and serve it over grilled chicken breasts.

¼ cup water

1 pint gooseberries, washed and drained

6 apricots—halved and pitted

1 pound bing cherries—pitted

¼ cup sugar

⅛ cup lemon verbena leaves—minced

In a 2-quart saucepan, add all of the ingredients and bring to a simmer over a medium flame. Lower the flame and cook the mixture for 20 minutes. Serve hot or cold over ice cream, pound cake, or angel food cake.

BEVERAGES

BLACK MINT JULEP

YIELDS APPROXIMATELY 2 QUARTS

The only claim I can make about my Southern heritage is that I spent my first year of life there, and so I beg the South's indulgence on this classic cooler. Black mint is a spearmint variety that has extremely dark green leaves that are considerably less ruffled than spearmint and a stem that is brownish-black in color. Its flavor is the strongest of mints that I have come across, with an aromatic bouquet that fills the house upon entering.

1 bunch black mint (or any mint variety available to you)

1 quart plus 1 pint water

2 cups sugar

2½ cups bourbon

1 cup brandy

Pull enough stem tops off the mint to use as a garnish, and reserve.

In a 2-quart sauce pot, add the water and sugar along with the stems of the black mint. Break up and add the mint leaves and stems to release the most flavor. Bring to a full simmer over a medium flame. Simmer 15 minutes, and then strain the fragrant water into a pitcher. Discard the stems. Add the bourbon and brandy into the pitcher and stir to combine.

Serve over ice in tall glass with a sprig of mint as garnish.

FRUIT SMOOTHIE

YIELDS APPROXIMATELY 4 CUPS

These blended drinks have such great diversity. I have made them for a quick breakfast, an after-workout shake, or a poolside cooler. I am constantly changing the fruits I use as the seasons change. It is best to use the ripest, freshest fruit you can find to give the smoothie as much flavor and sweetness as possible. If you want to up the ante in these smoothies, add a splash of dark rum into the blender.

    1 cup soy milk

    1 cup plain nonfat yogurt

    10 ice cubes

    1 ripe mango—peeled, pitted, and roughly chopped

    2 riped peaches—pitted and roughly chopped

    1 tablespoon honey

Place all of the ingredients in a blender and process until completely smooth.

VINEGARS AND OILS

CHERRY VINEGAR
YIELDS APPROXIMATELY 2 QUARTS

Never before have I made a vinegar that has made me so happy. Other vinegars such as raspberry excite me with their faint fruitiness, but this vinegar is not shy at all. The cherry scent will knock you out and the flavor will sing long after the season has faded.

½ **pound cherries**

2 quarts raw apple cider vinegar

Wash the cherries well and pat dry. Split the cherries in half and place in a 3- or 4-quart glass jar (pits and all). Pour the vinegar over the cherries and seal tightly. Place in a cool, dark spot for 3 weeks. During the second week, remove the lid on the vinegar, and with a large, clean spoon, push down on the cherries. This helps to release a bit more of their flavor. Reseal and let sit for the additional week. Strain the vinegar through a clean coffee filter or a few layers of cheesecloth into a clean glass jar, cover with a tight-fitting lid, and store in the refrigerator. It will last 6 months.

LEMON VERBENA VINEGAR

YIELDS 2 QUARTS

Notes

I probably can wax poetically for hours on the olfactory virtue of my favorite herb, lemon verbena—and I have been accused of such. Its powerfully aromatic scent fills me with all the glory of summer, and its versatility as an herb helps find its way into many a dish. This South American native gets tossed with fresh fruits, blended into fish marinades, stands guard as sweet potatoes bake, and mingles with champagne for a summer sorbet.

Basically I use old remnants of white wine for this vinegar. After a dinner party or two I usually have enough. This is going to be a very low acidic vinegar when it is done, which highlights beautifully the ethereal pleasure of the lemon verbena. The raw unfiltered vinegar is important here as is contains a "mother"—the yeast that promotes the fermenting of vinegar. Ver jus is juice made from the processing of underripe grapes and is now being produced locally in California and Long Island's North Fork and can be found in specialty and gourmet shops.

½ **pound fresh lemon verbena—washed and dried**

750 milliliter bottle ver jus

1 cup raw, unfiltered apple cider vinegar

4 cups white wine

Pack the lemon verbena in a 4-quart glass jar, bruising it liberally—this allows flavor to seep out more readily. Pour the ver jus, vinegar, and wine over the verbena. Cover with a tight-fitting lid and store in a dark, cool spot for 1 to 2 months (since I don't have a basement, I store mine in the refrigerator). Strain through a sieve lined with a clean coffee filter or cheesecloth into clean glass jars. Cover with a tight fitting lid and store in the refrigerator. It will last 6 months.

BLACK MINT OIL

The idea for this oil was borne out of a conversation I had with a masseur. He liked to use mint oil and had just ran out. I told him I'd make him some. The oils used here may also be used in a culinary application, since all the oils are edible. Besides easing aching muscles, try it with cherry vinegar for a fresh, bright vinaigrette drizzled over beets or as part of a marinade for lamb. If this variety of mint is unavailable to you, try spearmint or peppermint instead.

3 bunches black mint (about ¼ pound)

3 cups sweet almond oil

1 cup apricot kernel oil

½ cup mild-flavored olive oil

Wash the mint and set it to dry for a few hours on a clean kitchen towel.

Roughly chop the mint, stems and all, and place in a 3-quart glass jar. Pour over the oils and place in the refrigerator for 3 to 4 weeks with a tight-fitting seal. The oil will congeal somewhat in the refrigerator. Remove from the refrigerator and allow the oil to sit at room temperature for 1 hour to bring it back to a liquid state. Pour the oil through a strainer lined with a few layers of cheesecloth. Gather up the ends of the cheesecloth after the oil has strained through and wring out any excess oil. Store in the refrigerator for up to 6 months.

GARDEN PICKLE

YIELDS 1 GALLON JAR

I always crave those jars of pickled vegetables I walk past in the grocery store but find the look of their commercially produced jars to be so unappealing. So, finally after suffering an unfulfilled desire for too long, I decided one late-summer day to put up my own. The great thing is you can personalize the flavors by using the herbs that excite you most or removing the chili pepper if heat is not your thing.

1 head cauliflower—cut into florets

1 head broccoli—cut into florets

2 carrots—cut into ½-inch rounds

4 cloves garlic—skin peeled, whole

2 small zucchini—cut into ½-inch rounds

5 stalks celery—cut into 2-inch long pieces

2 onions—quartered

1 chili pepper—such as a jalapeño or habanero

10 black peppercorns

2 tablespoons salt

5 sprigs thyme

5 sprigs winter savory (or rosemary)

3 cups white wine vinegar

3 cups cold water

Bring a 4-quart pot of water to a boil, and blanch the cauliflower, broccoli, carrots, and garlic for 3 minutes. Drain and rinse under cold water. Let it sit for 15 minutes to drain off any excess water.

Place them, along with all of the remaining ingredients—except the vinegar and water—in a 1-gallon jar, and then add the vinegar and water. Cover with a nonmetallic lid, and refrigerate for 4 to 5 days before you start eating. The nonmetallic lid prevents the transference of a metalic flavor into the pickle. If you don't have a nonmetallic lid, place some plastic wrap over the top of the jar before you place the lid on. This keeps for a few months in the refrigerator—if it doesn't get eaten up immediately.

MEXICAN PICKLE

YIELDS ABOUT 2 QUARTS

After leaving the West Coast and moving back to the New York area, I missed many things. One was the chips and pickles I got at my favorite Mexican restaurant in the Mission District of San Francisco. This is the best duplication of the pickles I was able to come up with. As for the chips . . . I get them shipped in.

Notes

If you can secure fresh bay leaves, use them; their flavor is so much more pronounced than the dried leaves. The extra bay leaves freeze very well wrapped in plastic for about 3 months.

2 medium carrots—peeled and cut into 4-inch long sticks

$\frac{1}{2}$ pound jicama root—peeled and sliced into 4-inch long sticks

1 small onion—peeled and sliced thin

1 jalapeño pepper—pierced a few times with a knife

2 garlic cloves—skinned, whole

1 bay leaf

$1\frac{1}{2}$ cup white vinegar

2 limes—juiced

$1\frac{1}{2}$ cups water

Place the carrots, jicama, onion, jalapeño peppers, garlic clove, and bay leaf snugly into a 2-quart jar. (I use a 1-liter jar with a rubber-lined lid or line the top with plastic wrap). Add the vinegar, lime juice, and water to cover the vegetables. Add additional vinegar and water, if needed, to cover the vegetables.

Refrigerate for 3 days before you start eating them.

Summer starts its cooling fade
My garden, refuses to be thwarted
In packets I collect seeds

NOTES

NOTES

NOTES

AUTUMN

Walking through the park
another season falls
Tomorrow, I'll cook a stew

❧ AUTUMN'S BOUNTY ❧

As the brilliant light of summer starts to fade and the days grow shorter, markets start filling up with tough-skinned squashes, tightly bound brussels sprouts, and crisp apples. For most of us, these are the flavors and textures of autumn and throughout the winter.

Vegetables	Herbs	Fruits
Acorn squash	Chervil	Apples
Arugula	Chives	Asian pears
Beets	Dill	Cantaloupe
Brussels sprouts	Mint	Grape
Broccoli rabe	Parsley	Grapefruit
Cabbage	Rosemary	Kiwi
Carrots	Sage	Lemons
Cauliflower	Savory	Oranges
Celery	Tarragon	Pears
Celery root	Thyme	Pecans
Chicory		Persimmons
Collards		Pomegranate
Garlic		Quince
Horseradish		Walnuts
Kale		
Leeks		
Mushrooms		
Olives		
Onions		
Parsnips		
Pistachio		
Pumpkin		
Rutabagas		
Shelling beans		
Soy beans		
Squash (hard-skinned)		
Sweet potatoes		
Swiss chard		
Turnips		

Variety	Description	Use
Blue Hubbard	Solid yellow flesh, well-flavored.	Boiled, baked, in casseroles, excellent for pies.
Baby's delight	Intense orange color and highest Vitamin C content of all squashes plus high in carotene. Developed especially for baby food.	Boiled, baked, in soups, purees. Excellent for pies.
Best cheese	Dark orange flesh.	Ultimate pumpkin pie.
Buttercup	Extra rich and sweet in flavor. Deep orange flesh is firm and smooth. High in carotene.	Baked, pureed, stuffed, in casseroles.
White acorn	Pale yellow flesh is very smooth with delicate sweet flavor, free of pumpkin taste. High in calcium.	Baked, stuffed, boiled.
Green acorn	Thick, bright orange flesh. Smooth and delicious.	Baked, stuffed, boiled.
Golden acorn	Bright orange flesh, very delicious.	Baked, stuffed, boiled.
Stripetti	Cross between delicata and spaghetti squash. Excellent flavor.	Baked, stuffed, boiled.

Sugar pumpkin	Firm, high-quality sweet flesh.	Excellent for pies, cookies, cakes, breads, and soups.
Sweet dumpling	Very sweet, tender orange flesh.	Excellent for baking and stuffing. Ideal as a single serving.
Delicata	Very sweet orange flesh.	Excellent for baking and stuffing.
Sugarloaf	Delicata-type winter squash.	Stuffing and baking.

STARTERS

This salsa has great diversity. It complements chicken, turkey, wild rice, and even potato pancakes.

APPLE PEAR SALSA

YIELDS APPROXIMATELY 4 CUPS

When creating a salsa, I find that the finer I dice the ingredients, the more attractive the finished sauce looks and tastes. This is especially true with the ginger root in this recipe; too large a dice will overpower any palate. Given that these are raw sauces, dicing finely helps produce small explosions on your tongue.

2 Granny Smith apples—peeled and cored

2 pears—peeled and cored

1 pomegranate—juice only (about $1/2$ cup)

$1/4$ cup fresh lemon juice

$1/4$ cup fresh lime juice

1 small red onion—diced fine

2-inch long piece of ginger root—peeled and diced fine

1 tablespoon fresh thyme—chopped

1 tablespoon fresh Italian parsley—chopped

2 tablespoons fresh chives—chopped

White pepper and salt to taste

Dice the apples and pears and toss with the pomegranate, lemon, and lime juices. Toss in with the remaining ingredients, and let sit 1 hour before using.

PEAR CHUTNEY

YIELDS APPROXIMATELY 3 CUPS

I have been curious for years about using vanilla in savory applications, especially since it is one of my favorite flavors. The whole experiment started by accident when I was having dinner at a friend's one summer evening and we needed a sauce for the grilled vegetable plate. The pantry was limited, but there was vanilla extract, and since the idea had been rumbling through my thoughts, I threw caution to the wind and made a lime and vanilla vinaigrette . . . it worked beautifully.

1 tablespoon olive oil

1 onion—diced

5 pears (such as bosc or anjou)—peeled, cored, and cut into ¼-inch cubes

½ cup white wine

1 vanilla pod—split in half

¼ teaspoon nutmeg—preferably freshly grated

4 stems fresh rosemary—chopped

Salt and freshly ground black pepper to taste

In a 2-quart saucepan, heat the oil over a medium flame and add the onions. Cook for about 10 minutes until the onions start to caramelize. Add the pears, and cook another 5 minutes. Pour in the white wine and the other remaining ingredients, and let it come to a boil. Reduce the heat to a simmer, and let it cook for about 1 hour. If the mixture starts to get dry, add a little water to prevent the chutney from burning.

Notes
Serve this sauce as an accompaniment to Thanksgiving dinner.

QUINCE AND POMEGRANATE CHUTNEY

YIELDS APPROXIMATELY 3 CUPS

The chutney is an Indian condiment that employs sweet, sour, and spicy elements in the sauce. It develops well in the refrigerator over time as the flavors mellow somewhat and marry together. This chutney gives a nod to its Indian origins. However, the quince and pomegranate are indigenous to ancient Persia.

1 tablespoon canola oil

1 small onion, chopped

2 garlic cloves—chopped

1½ pounds quince—peeled, cored, and cut into ½-inch cubes

¼-inch long piece ginger—peeled and diced finely

1 chili pepper—seeded and diced (such as Asian, serrano, or jalapeno)

¼ cup white wine

2 tablespoons cider vinegar

Salt and black pepper to taste

1 pomegranate—seeds only

In a 2-quart saucepan, heat the oil over a medium flame and add the onion. Cook the onion until it is translucent, about 5 minutes. Then add the garlic and ginger, cooking for 1 to 2 minutes.

Add the quince along with the chili pepper, white wine, vinegar, salt and pepper. Cook the mixture, covered, over a low flame, for 45 minutes. Correct seasoning. Mix in the pomegranate seeds.

Serve this chutney with roasted chicken or with a slice of sharp white cheddar cheese, crusty bread, and a glass of port.

VANILLA PEAR SAUCE

YIELDS APPROXIMATELY 2 CUPS

There is an absolute elegance to this unexpected sauce that complements roast pork, game, or even the Thanksgiving turkey. The variety of pear here is not so important, since it gets cooked down to the consistency of applesauce. You want underripe pears since they will not overpower this concoction with too sugary of a palate.

2 tablespoons walnut oil

2 shallots—diced fine

¼ cup ver jus

⅛ teaspoon clove—ground

⅛ teaspoon nutmeg—ground

1 vanilla bean—split in half lengthwise

4 underripe pears—peeled, cored, and cut into ½-inch cubes

Salt and freshly ground black pepper to taste

Heat a 2-quart saucepan over a medium flame and add the walnut oil and shallots. Cook for about 3 to 4 minutes, until the shallots lose their raw look. Add the ver jus, clove, nutmeg, and vanilla bean, and reduce the liquid by half, about 4 to 5 minutes. Add the pears and combine well. Cook, covered, over a medium-low flame for 20 minutes. Discard the vanilla bean and season with salt and pepper. Serve this sauce either hot or cold.

PUMPKIN SOUP

YIELDS 6 SERVINGS

This American native gourd is clearly our icon food. The burnt orange skin immediately puts one in an autumnal state of mind. There are a plethora of pumpkin varieties available, and I recommend trying them all. While I was living in Australia I discovered the Hubbard blue, a wonderful meaty variety with a dusty-blue gray skin that I often use when making this soup. In this country I see this pumpkin variety referred to simply as a Hubbard.

> 2 tablespoons unsalted butter
>
> 1 large onion—diced
>
> 2 garlic cloves—rougly chopped
>
> 4 cups pumpkin—chopped
>
> 3 carrots—peeled and diced
>
> ½ teaspoon nutmeg—ground
>
> ⅛ teaspoon clove—ground
>
> 2 quarts chicken or vegetable stock
>
> Salt and freshly ground black pepper to taste

In a 6-quart saucepan, melt the butter over a medium flame and add the onion and garlic. Cook until the onion turns translucent, about 4 to 5 minutes. Add the pumpkin, carrots, nutmeg, clove, and stock. Bring to a boil and then reduce to a simmer. Cook the soup 30 to 45 minutes until the pumpkin and carrots are tender.

Place the soup in the bowl of the food processor and blend until smooth. Return to the saucepan and bring back to a boil. Correct seasoning with salt and pepper and serve with Chili Cream.

Chili Cream

1 cup sour cream or plain yogurt

1 lime—juiced

2 teaspoons cumin—ground

1 teaspoon cayenne pepper

Salt and black pepper to taste

Mix all ingredients together and let sit 30 minutes.

GINGER BUTTERNUT SOUP

YIELDS 8 SERVINGS

Any time you a use a blender to puree a hot liquid, never fill the jar more than one-third full. The pressure created by the steam tends to cause the lid to come lose, and you can be sorely burned. So puree this soup in small batches or use a handheld blending wand if you have one. The food processor is also an option, just keep blending the soup with an on-off pulse to get a smooth finished soup.

1 tablespoon canola oil

1 medium onion—roughly chopped

2 leeks—whites only, chopped

1 fennel bulb—roughly chopped (approx. 1 cup)

2 garlic cloves—diced

2-inch long piece of ginger root—peeled and chopped

1 teaspoon coriander—ground

3 cups vegetable or chicken stock

3 pounds butternut squash—peeled, seeded, and cut into 1-inch pieces

2 carrots—peeled and chopped

Salt and black pepper to taste

Heat in a 2-quart pot over medium-high flame and add the canola oil, onion, leeks, and fennel. Cook until they lose their raw look, about 4 to 5 minutes. Add the garlic, ginger, and coriander and cook for an additional 3 minutes. Add the remaining ingredients and bring to a boil. Reduce the heat to a simmer, and cook for 30 minutes or until the butternut squash is fork-tender.

Puree the soup in a blender until smooth and return to the pot, correct seasoning, and keep warm.

Serve this soup with a salad of bitter greens with a vinaigrette made with Cherry Vinegar (page 113) and crusty peasant bread.

BEANS AND ROASTED VEGETABLE SOUP

YIELDS 12 SERVINGS

What is more satisfying on a cold day than a pot of soup simmering away on the stove, filling the house with sweet-earthy notes that promise contentment and a satiated stomach? This recipe takes you through winter. It uses all those root vegetables that wait in the cellar to be called into action. Feel free to add potatoes, mushrooms, or celery root into this soup as the inspiration strikes you. Chances are, the rutabaga you'll purchase will be covered in a food-grade wax, which helps aid its shelf-life. If so, omit its skin from the stock base, as it will melt and add an oily feel.

Note

This is one of those soups that age fabulously. Days 3 and 4 are better than the first. I only recommend adding fresh parsley with each serving, since its flavor fades so quickly.

3 heads garlic

3 carrots (about ¼ pound)

3 parsnips (about ½ pound)

1 large turnip (about ½ pound)

1 large rutabaga (about 1 pound)

5 stalks celery

2 large leeks

2 large onions

2 large fennel bulbs

5 bay leaves

10 black peppercorns

1 cup parsley leaves—tightly packed, stems reserved

4 quarts water

¼ cup olive oil

2 cups white navy beans

1 cup split green peas

1 cup brown lentils

Salt and freshly ground black pepper to taste

Tabasco sauce (optional)

Preheat the oven to 350°F.

Cut the stem tops off the garlic bulbs, rub the garlic with a small amount of olive oil, and wrap in aluminum foil. Bake the garlic for about 45 minutes or until it is very soft to the touch. Cool slightly, and then squeeze out the soft pulp from the skin.

Reserve both the skin and pulp separately.

Peel and dice all the vegetables into ½-inch cubes. Reserve all the vegetable peelings to the side.

In an 8-quart stockpot, combine all the reserved vegetable peelings, the roasted garlic skin, 2 of the bay leaves, the peppercorns, and parsley stems (reserving the leaves), and cover with the water. Bring to a boil over a high heat, and then reduce heat to a simmer. Cook for 1 hour. Shut off heat, and let the stock sit for 1 hour before straining and discarding the vegetable peelings. Cool the stock completely.

Preheat the oven to 400°F.

Coat the cubed vegetables with the olive oil and then roast on baking trays until golden brown. This will take approximately 20 to 30 minutes.

While the vegetables are roasting, bring the stock back to a boil over a hight heat and add all the beans, roasted garlic, and remaining 3 bay leaves. Reduce heat to simmer. When the vegetables are done, add to the stock base. Use a little stock to lift up (deglaze) any particles that may have stuck to the trays. Add that to the stock base. Simmer for 2 hours. Season with salt and pepper and, if desired, some Tabasco sauce. Add the parsley, chopped, just prior to serving.

If the soup gets too thick, add some additional water.

STUFFED DUMPLING SQUASH

YIELDS 8 SERVINGS

The Black Twig apple in this recipe is admittedly an obscure variety, but it is extremely crisp and sweet with a lovely hint of tartness. If I don't get to the market early in the morning, they're gone. Any firm apple can be used in its place here. Also, try adding some smoked turkey or chicken sausage into the recipe.

   8 small dumpling squash or Jack-be-Little pumpkins

   1 fennel bulb

   2 carrots

   3 Black Twig apples (or any firm sweet apple)

   ⅛ cup lemon thyme leaves—chopped

   ¼ cup white wine

   Salt and freshly ground black pepper to taste

Cut the squash at its top to create a lid. Carefully scoop out the seed and pulp pocket and discard.

Preheat the oven to 350°F.

Dice the fennel, carrots, and apples very fine, and toss with the lemon thyme, wine, salt and pepper. Stuff the squash with the filling and replace the lid. Place in a 15 x 9 roasting pan. Fill the pan with enough water to come one-quarter of the way up the squash. Place in the oven and bake 30 to 45 minutes, or until tender. Serve immediately.

PUMPKIN GNOCCHI WITH GORGONZOLA SAUCE

YIELDS 8 TO 10 SERVINGS

When I was on the Amalfi coast, I had a dish of eggplant gnocchi tossed with cherry tomatoes, basil, and olive oil. Gnocchi from eggplant . . . it got me thinking. If you have made gnocchi before from potato, this dough is going to seem a little more moist. I recommend having a small pot of water boiling so you can cook and test the gnocchi. The cooked gnocchi should contain enough flour to bind it but not too much to make it feel like a lead pellet going down.

> 3 cups cooked pumpkin meat (approx. 3-pound pumpkin or canned)
>
> 2 to 3 cups all-purpose flour
>
> 3 large eggs
>
> ¼ cup olive oil
>
> 1 teaspoon nutmeg—ground
>
> 2 tablespoons salt

Preheat the oven to 350°F.

If you are using a fresh pumpkin, slice the top off and remove the seeds. Bake the pumpkin in the oven for 30 to 45 minutes, or until fork-tender. Scoop out the pumpkin meat and mash to a smooth mixture. Lay it out on a baking tray and return it to the oven for 15 minutes to evaporate any excess moisture. Remove from the oven and allow it to cool slightly.

Place the pumpkin meat on a clean work surface and make a large well in the middle. Sprinkle about 1¼ cups of the flour over the pumpkin. In the well, add the eggs, olive oil, nutmeg, and salt and gently beat it to combine. Mix the pumpkin/flour into the egg mixture, blending it all together. If the gnocchi mixture feels wet and tacky, continue to work in additonal flour utnil the dough mass is not tacky to the touch.

Divide the pumpkin dough mass into 6 pieces. Roll each piece into a log approximiately 1-inch round. Cut the log into ½-inch pieces. You can either lightly pinch the gnocchi or you may lightly roll the piece up the back of the fork to create some ridges. Hold the gnocchi on a clean, well-floured kitchen towel as you make them so they don't end up sticking to your work surface. Freeze, or cook the gnocchi in a large quantity of boiling water until it floats to the surface, about 4 to 5 minutes. Serve immediately.

Gorgonzola Cream Sauce

> **3 cups cream**
>
> **⅛ cup brandy**
>
> **1 tablespoon thyme leaves—roughly chopped**
>
> **2 teaspoons Dijon mustard**
>
> **⅛ pound Gorgonzola cheese—crumbled**
>
> **Salt and black pepper to taste**

In a saucepan, bring the cream, brandy, thyme, and mustard to a boil. Reduce to a simmer and cook until reduced by half in volume, about 15 minutes. Whisk in the Gorgonzola and add the salt and pepper. Spoon over the gnocchi and serve. This makes about 2 cups.

DUCK CONFIT CROQUETTES
YIELDS APPROXIMATELY 16 CROQUETTES

"Confit" comes from the French word meaning "preserve." In days of old, the process of cooking fowl in its rendered fat and then storing it submerged in that fat in the cellar helped guarantee meat through the lean winter months. This is a wonderfully rich and flavorful way of curing the duck, though fortunately you do not have to do it yourself any longer. In many markets I have found that the purveyor of wild fowl is doing it for me. If you do not have such a purveyor, try your butcher or one of the many mail-order game-food distributors around the country.

1 pound shredded duck confit

4 egg whites—lightly beaten

2 whole large eggs—lightly beaten

2 cups bread crumbs

4 shallots—finely diced

2 tablespoons thyme leaves—chopped

2 tablespoons Italian parsley leaves—chopped

2 garlic cloves—crushed to a paste

2 tablespoons olive oil

Mix the duck, eggs whites, whole eggs, 1¼ cup of the bread crumbs, shallots, thyme, parsley, and garlic together to thoroughly distribute. The mixture should be moist and, when squeezed, hold its form. Using about a ¼ cup of the duck mixture, form into golf-ball-size rounds (croquettes) and then slightly flatten. Carefully toss the croquettes in the remaining ¾ cup of bread crumbs.

Heat a 10-inch sauté pan over a high heat, and add the oil and half the croquettes. Cook on each side for 2 to 3 minutes until golden brown. Then transfer onto an absorbent paper towel and cook the remaining croquettes. Serve two croquettes warm per person on a bed of greens with Apple Pear Salsa (page 128).

For hours we toil
Roasting; Slicing autumn's feast
With a prayer we eat

SMOKED SALMON, ROASTED BEETS, GOAT CHEESE, AND MARINATED RED ONIONS WITH CITRUS VINAIGRETTE

YIELDS 6 SERVINGS

This is a very successful first course, and all the elements can be easily prepared well in advance of serving. I would not assemble the plate too far in advance though, since the beets will leak out their dark red color. You may want to add some Belgium endive to the salad if serving it as a lunch course.

1 large red onion

$\frac{1}{2}$ cup champagne vinegar or lemon verbena vinegar (page 114)

3 beets (approx $\frac{3}{4}$ pound)

$\frac{1}{4}$ cup water

11-ounce log goat cheese

$\frac{1}{4}$ cup dill leaves—chopped

$\frac{1}{2}$ pound smoked salmon—sliced thin

$\frac{1}{2}$ cup whole walnuts—light toasted

12 croutons

Cut the onion in half through the root, and then slice the onion paper thin. Toss the sliced onion with the champagne vinegar and let sit for 30 minutes to 1 hour.

Preheat the oven to 350°F.

Wrap the beet in aluminum foil, drizzled with the water, and place in the oven. Bake for 30 to 45 minutes until fork-tender. Cool slightly and then rub the skin off the beets. Slice the beets into $\frac{1}{4}$-inch thin rounds.

Place the goat cheese in the freezer for 30 minutes. It is easier to slice the cheese if it's firm. Slice the goat cheese into 12 pieces and roll in the chopped dill.

Assemble the plate by placing three slices of smoked salmon on the plate along the outer perimeter. In the center, place the marinated onions, sliced beets and the goat cheese sitting on top of the croutons. Drizzle with citrus vinaigrette and garnish with walnuts.

Citrus Vinaigrette

> ¼ cup fresh orange juice
>
> 1 tablespoon Dijon mustard
>
> Salt and black pepper to taste
>
> ¾ cup olive oil

Mix the orange juice, mustard, salt and pepper together to blend. Then slowly whisk in the oil. This makes about 1 cup.

SMOKED TROUT SALAD

YIELDS 4 SERVINGS

I love this scrumptious salad plate. There is a fantastic harmony created by the smokiness of the trout, the sweet tang of the apples, and the earthiness of the celery root—all blanketed with the saltiness of the blue cheese dressing. The Matsu apple is a very crisp, tart apple; however, a Granny Smith apple will be an absolutely acceptable substitution.

1 head frissee lettuce (chicory)

½ pound smoked trout

1 small celery root

⅛ cup apple cider vinegar

1 Matsu apple (or other tart apple)

1 red pepper—roasted, skinned, and julienned

Wash the head of lettuce, but keep the leaves intact.

Flake the smoked trout.

Slice the celery root a very fine julienne, and then toss in apple cider vinegar to prevent it from turning brown.

Slice the apple thinly, and also hold in some water to prevent them from browning.

Assemble the salad by placing some of the frissee greens on a plate. Sprinkle some trout along with some celery root and red pepper. Fan the apples on the side of the plate. Drizzle with dressing. Serve.

Blue Cheese Dressing

⅛ pound blue cheese

2 tablespoons Dijon mustard

¼ cup sherry vinegar

⅛ cup chives—chopped

¼ cup walnut oil

Salt and freshly ground black pepper to taste

Make the dressing by placing all the dressing ingredients in the food processor and blending until smooth and incorporated. Correct seasoning. Makes about 1 cup.

MAIN COURSES

VENISON SAUSAGE STEW
YIELDS 12 SERVINGS

Notes
If game is not your thing, you can easily substitute any full-flavor sausage in this recipe, such as Cajun andouille, lamb, or duck sausage.

Burdock and salsify are two root vegetables that are sorely underused in this country. They have a sweet woodsy taste and are at their best if harvested after the first cold snap of the season (ugh, snow can't be far behind). Burdock can grow up to 3 feet in length, whereas salsify is a less intimidating 9 to 12 inches. I use these vegetables interchangeably depending on availability. However, I can usually find burdock in Japanese markets (they called it gobo).

3 tablespoons unsalted butter

3 tablespoons all-purpose flour

1 large onion—diced

1 to 2 habanero chili peppers—seeded and diced

2 large carrots—diced into 1-inch cubes

$\frac{1}{2}$ pound quince—peeled, cored, and quartered

1 pound new potatoes (golf-ball size)

$\frac{1}{2}$ pound celery root—peeled and cut into $\frac{1}{2}$-inch cubes

$\frac{1}{4}$ pound burdock root—peeled and cut into $\frac{1}{2}$-inch rounds

$\frac{1}{2}$ cup savory leaves—chopped

$\frac{1}{4}$ cup thyme leaves—chopped

$\frac{1}{4}$ cup Italian parsley leaves—chopped

2 cups tomato juice

$1\frac{1}{2}$ pounds venison sausage

1 cup red wine

Salt and black pepper to taste

In a 4-quart heavily lined casserole dish, melt the butter over medium heat and add the flour. Cook the mixture, stirring constantly until it darkens to a light brown. This is a roux, which will help thicken the stew and add flavor. This will take about 10 minutes, though you must remember to keep the butter mixture moving in order not to burn it. Add the onion, habanero pepper, carrots, and quince. Continue cooking for 5 minutes. Add the potatoes, celery root, burdock root, and half the amount of herbs. Pour in the tomato juice, scrape the bottom of the pot, and allow the ingredients to slowly come to a boil over a medium-low heat.

In a separate 10-inch sauté pan, cook the sausage over a high heat to firm up and crisp on the outside. Remove the sausage from the sauté pan, reserving on absorbent paper towels, and pour the red wine into the pan to deglaze—to pick up all the wonderful "brown bits" adhering to the bottom of the pan. Reduce the red wine by half, which will take about 3 to 5 minutes, and then pour it into the stew. Cut the sausage into $\frac{1}{2}$-inch pieces and add to the stew. Taste and season with salt and pepper. Let the stew simmer for 45 minutes. Add the remaining herbs, salt and pepper, and cook an additional 15 minutes. Serve steaming hot with Fennel Salad (page 168).

SALMON AND AROMATIC
VEGETABLES IN PAPILLOTE

YIELDS 6 SERVINGS

Serving and opening something wrapped in paper like this creates a wondrous fume of aromatics that is gentle and inviting. Take the parcels right from the oven to the table and allow each diner to open his own and catch a whiff of the heady scent. You can do most fish in this style, as well as boneless chicken breast or vegetables. Chicken will take about 20 minutes while the vegetables will only take about 10 minutes. All the vegetables should be cut very thin, or alternatively, you can blanch them in boiling water to ensure that they will be cooked.

Parchment paper

¼ cup canola oil

6 5-ounce salmon fillets

2 shallots—sliced thinly

2 carrots—peeled and julienned

1 fennel bulb—julienned

1 medium red onion—sliced thinly

2 limes—juiced

Salt and freshly ground black pepper to taste

Preheat the oven to 425°F.

Cut 5 8-inch rounds of parchment paper. Fold each in half to create a seam, and then unfold the circle. Grease one-half with some of the canola oil. Lay a fillet down, on the oiled side, and sprinkle with some shallots, carrots, fennel, red onion, and lime juice. Season with salt and pepper. Fold the empty half of the parchment over the fillet and crimp the edge tightly closed. Place in the oven for 15 minutes, and serve immediately in its paper.

FLOUNDER ENCASED IN CRISP DESIREE POTATOES

YIELDS 4 SERVINGS

This is a recipe where, if you have a mandolin (a standing French table slicer available in specialty stores), you might want to break it out in order to get the potatoes nice and thin. Otherwise, slow and steady with a very sharp knife will get you there. The Desiree potato, native to the northeast, is sweet with a slightly variegated flesh. You could just as easily use Yukon Gold potatoes.

**1 pound Desiree potatoes—large in size in order to get
   pieces that cover the fillet**

½ cup olive oil

1 pound flounder fillet

Salt and freshly ground black pepper

¼ cup fennel leaves—roughly chopped

Preheat the oven to 375°F.

Slice the potatoes into ⅛-inch thick rounds. Heat the olive oil in a 10-inch sauté pan over a high heat, and cook the potatoes to golden and crisp on each side, about 5 minutes total. Remove from the pan. On a baking tray, lay a single layer of the crisped potatoes wide enough to serve as a bed for the flounder fillet. Lay the flounder down; sprinkle with salt and pepper and fennel leaves. Lay another layer of potatoes on top of the flounder. Bake for 15 minutes. Carefully lift the flounder from the tray with a spatula and transfer to a plate, and serve immediately with Kale with Carmelized Onions and Portobello Mushrooms (page 161).

SAUTÉED CHILEAN SEA BASS WITH CHAMPAGNE GRAPES

YIELDS 6 SERVINGS

I remember the first time I ate a sauce that contained grapes. I thought, "Yikes, what's going on here?" I quickly came to love the mingling of sweet, sour, and salty, and now readily seek it out. The champagne grapes are a small variety now found around the country in mid-autumn. They have a brilliant sweetness and are charmingly petite in size. If I can't get these diminutive grapes, I prefer to use red flame grapes for the color contrast they offer.

2 pounds Chilean sea bass fillets

¼ cup all-purpose flour

Salt and freshly ground black pepper to taste—to season the flour

3 tablespoons olive oil

2 shallots—finely diced

1 red Asian chili—seeded and finely diced

1 garlic clove—diced

¼ cup ver jus

½ cup white wine

1 tablespoon thyme leaves—roughly chopped

2 tablespoons chives—chopped

½ cup champagne grapes—all stems removed

2 tablespoons unsalted butter—at room temperature

Salt and pepper to taste

Preheat the oven to 250°F.

Cut the bass into 6 pieces. Dredge the fish in the flour that has been seasoned with salt and pepper.

Heat a 12-inch sauté pan over a high heat and add the olive oil. Cook the fish about 6 minutes until golden and cooked through, turning it over once. Remove from the pan and place onto a plate. Hold in the oven to keep warm.

Draw off the excess oil in the sauté pan, and return to the heat. Add the shallots and chili pepper cooking until the shallots just start to brown, about 3 minutes. Add the garlic and ver jus and reduce to a glaze. Pour in the white wine and thyme leaves and reduce the liquid by half. This will take about 8 minutes. Remove the pan from the heat, add the chives and grapes, and swirl in the butter. Season with salt and pepper. Immediately pour the sauce over the fish and serve.

ANCHO CHILI-RUBBED PORK TENDERLOIN FILLET

YIELDS 6 SERVINGS

This chili is the dried version of the pablano chili. In some parts of the United States, the ancho chili is referred to as a *pasilla*. It's an oblong pear shape with a dark brown color and an intense, raisin-like aroma. Store any additional chilies you may have bought in the freezer to help keep their fragrance and prevent them from drying out any further. The leftover marinade in this recipe can be used on any poultry or on flank steak, or try it on tuna.

4 ancho chilies

1 small onion—diced

1 lime—juiced

Zest of 1 orange

1/4 cup cider vinegar

4 garlic cloves

1/8 cup oregano—dried

1 tablespoon cumin—ground

2 teaspoon coriander—ground

1/2 teaspoon cloves—ground

Salt and black pepper to taste

1/2 cup olive oil

2 pounds pork Tenderloin—trimmed of any fat and sinew

Heat a 4-inch sauté pan over a medium-high heat and place the chilies in the pan and toast for 1 minute, turning them over once. Let cool, then split them open and discard the seeds and stem. Place the chili along with the onion, lime juice, orange zest, vinegar, garlic, oregano, cumin, coriander, clove, salt and pepper in a blender. Make a paste by processing until smooth. You will have more chili paste then you will need. Store the remaining chili paste in the refrigerator with some oil drizzled over the top to prevent mold from forming. Spread the chili paste over the pork loin and let it marinate for 3 hours to overnight.

Preheat the oven to 375°F.

Take the pork out of the refrigerator about 30 minutes prior to cooking. This will take the hard chill out of it and allow the pork to cook more evenly. Place it on a baking tray and cook in the oven for 20 minutes. Let the tenderloin rest 10 minutes before slicing. Serve with slices of limes and Rye Berry Salad (page 160).

ROCK CORNISH GAME HENS RUBBED WITH ROSEMARY, ORANGE, AND GARLIC

YIELDS 4 SERVINGS

This hybrid chicken usually weighs in at no more than 2 pounds each, which is a perfect individual serving. To remove the backbone from the hen, you will need a strong pair of kitchen scissors or a heavy sharp chef's knife. At the wide opening of the cavity, cut down one side of the hen and then down the other side. The joint by the drumstick is the toughest spot and if you find yourself struggling, move the scissors or knife just slightly, since you are probably trying to break through the thickest part of the bone.

> 4 garlic cloves—minced very fine
>
> 2 tablespoons rosemary leaves—chopped
>
> 2 oranges—juiced (about ¾ cup)
>
> ¼ cup olive oil
>
> Salt and freshly ground black pepper to taste
>
> 4 rock cornish game hens—split open, backbone removed

In a bowl mix the garlic, rosemary, orange juice, salt and pepper together. Rub into the hens and let sit 1 hour to overnight refrigerated in a shallow pan.

Preheat the oven to 400°F.

Remove the hens from the marinade and place on a baking tray, breast side up. Bake for 30 to 35 minutes until skin is crisp and when the thigh is pierced, the juices run clear. Serve a whole hen per person with Curried Brussels Sprouts (page 164).

BRAISED BRISKET OF BEEF
YIELDS 6 TO 8 SERVINGS

In a way, this recipe pays homage to my mother and her holiday braise. In another, it says I have wandered far from my Eastern European roots. Sure, the black radishes, parsnips and mushrooms hearken back to my younger days. But the use of the chipotle chili and quince offer a hybridization of flavor. The chipotle is a dried, smoked jalapeno that is incendiary. It is available dried or in cans slathered in a tomato sauce (adobo sauce). Whichever one you find will work in this recipe.

3½ pound brisket of beef—trimmed well of excess fat and sinew

Salt and freshly ground black pepper to taste

2 medium onions—sliced thin

¼ pound black radishes—peeled and julienned

3 garlic cloves—roughly chopped

3 celery ribs—diced ¼ inch

2 small parsnips—diced into ¼ inch rounds

1 quince—peeled, cored, and cut into ½-inch cubes

¼ pound mushrooms—stems discarded and quartered

2 chipotles—left whole

¾ cup seltzer water

5 plum tomatoes—skinned, seeded, and quartered

½ cup Italian parsley—leaves only, roughly chopped

Preheat the oven to 325°F.

Heat a 9-quart casserole pot or Dutch oven, wide enough to fit the brisket laying down flat, over a medium-high heat. Season the brisket with salt and pepper. Place the fattier side of the brisket down in the pan and sear to deep brown. No oil is needed, since the fat on the brisket should be sufficient. However, if you cut away the entire fat cap, add about ⅛ cup olive oil to the pan first. Flip the brisket over and sear the other side. Brisket will take about 4 to 5 minutes per side to sear. Remove the brisket to a platter. Then add the onions, radishes,

Notes
The black radish used in this recipe is also known as a winter radish. It has a black skin and mild-tasting white flesh. I like to slice it very thinly and drizzle it with olive oil, lemon juice, and salt to serve as an appetizer. I grew up on it—grated and tossed with warm rendered chicken fat, which then garnished a smear of chopped liver.

and garlic to the pan. Cook for 5 minutes, stirring occasionally, and then return the brisket to the pan on top of the onion mixture. Add the celery, parsnips, quince, mushrooms, chipotles, and seltzer.

Bring to a boil and reduce the heat to a simmer. Cover the pan with a lid or aluminum foil. Place the brisket in the oven and cook for 1 hour. After 1 hour flip the brisket over and add the quartered tomatoes. Recover and place back in the oven for 1½ to 2 hours longer.

Remove the brisket from the pan to a platter and hold. Don't slice the brisket for at least 30 minutes after removing it from the oven. This time will allow the juices to relax back into the meat. In the meantime, return the casserole pot to the stove top and add the Italian parsley to the braising juices and vegetables and bring to a boil over a medium heat. Reduce to concentrate the flavors. If you desire, remove the chipotles and discard. Taste and correct seasoning with salt and pepper. Slice the brisket against the grain of the meat and place on a platter. Spoon the reduced juices and vegetables on top. Serve immediately.

ON THE SIDE

SWEET POTATO BRAISED IN APPLE CIDER

YIELDS 4 TO 6 SERVINGS

This recipe is so easy. I set it up in a porcelain baking dish that can go from oven to table. I have altered the recipe a bit by removing the salt and pepper and sprinkling some brown sugar over the top prior to baking, creating a sweeter version. Both send me over the top.

2 pounds sweet potatoes—peeled and sliced into ½-inch rounds

12 ounces apple cider

⅛ cup mint leaves—chopped

Salt and freshly ground black pepper to taste

Preheat the oven to 350°F.

In an 8 x 8 baking dish, shingle the sweet potatoes in a single layer. Add the apple cider, sprinkle with the mint leaves, and season with salt and pepper. Cover with aluminum foil, and place in the oven for 30 minutes or until tender. Serve hot or at room temperature.

SWEET POTATO BRAISED WITH LEMON VERBENA

I have gone on about verbena in previous recipes so I will spare you another sermon on the subject—except to say that I always dry my own verbena in late August. If fresh verbena is not available to me for this recipe, I grab some from my jar. If you want to dry herbs, I suggest hanging them from a hanger in a closet (or any dark, cool spot) for 1 week. I have also frozen verbena fresh, and to my surprise, it survives fairly well.

> 2 pounds sweet potatoes—peeled and sliced into ½-inch thick rounds
>
> ½ cup lemon verbena—leaves only
>
> 1 cup fresh orange juice
>
> ⅛ cup champagne vinegar or Cherry Vinegar (page 113)
>
> Salt and freshly ground black pepper to taste

Preheat the oven to 350°F.

In an 8 x 8 baking dish, shingle the sweet potatoes and verbena leaves in a single layer so that the verbena is sandwiched between the potato. Add the orange juice and vinegar, and season with salt and pepper. Cover with foil, and place in the oven for 30 minutes or until tender. Serve hot.

ADZUKI BEANS AND ROASTED SWEET POTATOES

YIELDS 8 SERVINGS

The *ketcap manis* contained within this recipe is an Indonesian condiment, which is a sweet soy sauce. It is believed that this sauce is the origin of what we call ketchup. *Ketcap manis* can be found in most Asian markets and some Indian stores. Try to buy a *ketcap manis* that is made in Indonesia as opposed to a Dutch product—besides costing less, the flavor is much better.

¼ cup rice wine vinegar

2 quarts water

½-inch long piece ginger root—peeled and diced

2 cups adzuki beans—soaked overnight and drained

2 large sweet potatoes (approx. 1 pound)—peeled and diced into ¼-inch cubes

3 tablespoons sesame oil

1 red onion—peeled and diced

3 celery stalks—diced

½ cup cilantro—chopped

¼ cup *ketcap manis* or low-sodium soy sauce

Salt and freshly ground black pepper to taste

Toss the vinegar and ginger together, and let it marinate for 30 minutes.

In a 4-quart pot, bring the water to a boil over a high heat. Add the beans, and lower the heat to a simmer and cook for 30 minutes or until the beans are soft to the bite. Drain and hold.

Preheat the oven to 350°F.

Toss the sweet potatoes in the sesame oil, and lay on a baking tray. Oven-roast the potatoes for 20 to 25 minutes until they are soft and browned. For the last 5 minutes of the roasting, sprinkle the onions over the potatoes. When done, toss the potatoes and the other ingredients together in a large bowl. Serve hot.

Notes

This dish can be enjoyed warm or as a cold bean salad. If eating it cold, you may want to add some additional lemon juice or rice wine vinegar to the salad.

RYE BERRY SALAD

YIELDS 8 TO 12 SERVINGS

This is an unusual salad in so far as rye berries are not a commonly used grain, and yet they have a great nutty taste and good chewy texture. I tend to find freshly dried rye berries in the green market locally, but you can easily find them in most health-food stores. Jerusalem artichokes are not related to the artichoke at all; rather, they are cousin to the sunflower. The crisp, mild tuber is usually irregular and knobby in shape. I confess I search for the most uniform-shaped ones, since they are easier to peel and give me the least amount of waste. They are quite edible raw. However, try them boiled, added into stews, or sautéed.

1 pound rye berries

6 cups water

½ pound Jerusalem artichokes

¼ pound mixed sprouts (chick pea, lentil, and sweet pea)

½ pound baby spinach—washed and dried

1 small red onion—diced

⅛ cup savory—leaves only, chopped

⅛ cup thyme—leaves only, chopped

½ cup sherry vinegar

2 tablespoons Dijon mustard

¼ cup olive oil

Salt and black pepper to taste

Bring the rye berries and water to a boil over high heat in a 4-quart saucepan. Simmer for 30 minutes, or until tender to the bite. Peel and dice the Jerusalem artichokes into ¼-inch rounds, and mix with the sprouts, spinach, onion, savory, thyme, vinegar, mustard, and olive oil. When the rye berries are cooked, drain any excess water through a colander, and then toss the hot rye berries with the vegetable mixture. Add salt and pepper to taste. Let cool before serving. This salad is great the next day, served cold.

KALE WITH CARAMELIZED ONIONS AND PORTOBELLO MUSHROOMS

YIELDS 6 SERVINGS

The portobello mushroom started showing up more regularly over the last decade and is now found in most green markets and groceries. When you buy them, they should not have dried caps or gills that look very worn. I always cut the gills out from the underbelly of the cap, since they tend to leak moisture, which turns everything brown. The portobello is one of the meatiest mushrooms available, with a dense palate texture. It's a favorite addition to vegetarian sandwiches because it has such a satisfying mouth feel.

Notes

This dish is great on toasted peasant bread or as a bed for a piece of chicken.

1 pound kale

4 quarts water

¼ cup olive oil

1 large onion—sliced in ¼-inch slices

2 portobello mushrooms—sliced in ¼-inch strips

Salt and freshly ground black pepper to taste

Pull the leaves of the kale from the stem, and blanch in the boiling water for 2 minutes. Drain.

Over medium heat, add the olive oil into a 10-inch sauté pan. Add the onions and sauté until golden, about 15 minutes. Then add the mushrooms. Cook until the mushrooms soften, about 5 to 7 minutes. Toss the kale into the mushroom mixture and cook another 5 minutes. Season with salt and pepper. Serve hot.

CLOVE-SPICED BEET ROOT PUREE
YIELDS 6 SERVINGS

Right before I left Sydney, Australia, friends took me to lunch to a lovely restaurant about two hours out of the city on a little lake island. It was magical. One of the side dishes served was a peppery beet root puree. It was delicious but had too much pepper for my taste. So, upon coming home, I started to play with the idea. Clove gave the kick I wanted without leaving a burning effect. This a great side dish, but you can also use it to stuff mini-pumpkins, which you then bake. Serve one mini-pumpkin per person. The orange and red combination is groovy.

> 3 pounds beet root
>
> 2 ounces tomato paste
>
> 1½ teaspoons clove—ground
>
> Salt and freshly ground black pepper to taste

Wash the beets to dislodge any dirt clinging to its skins. Then place the beets in a 4-quart pot and cover generously with cold water. Over a high heat, bring the pot to a boil and cook the beets for 20 to 30 minutes, or until fork-tender. The older the beets, the longer they take to cook. Drain in a colander and allow to cool slightly. While still warm, rub the skin from the flesh of the beets—this should happen rather easily. Then roughly chop the beets.

In a food processor fitted with the steel blade, puree the still-warm beets until smooth.

In a 2-quart saucepan, sauté the tomato paste for 3 minutes over high heat, keeping it moving to prevent it from scorching. Add the beets, season with the clove, salt and pepper, and simmer over a low flame for 20 minutes to blend the flavors. Serve warm.

SWEET POTATO SOUFFLÉ

YIELDS 8 SERVINGS

Remember that Thanksgiving Day classic—the mini-marshmallow sweet potato casserole? Here I have elevated what was once a simple autumnal concoction to a greater moment. Have no fear, this is not the type of soufflé where you have to have everyone walk around on tiptoe or rush it to the table as soon as it comes out the oven before it sadly deflates. If persimmons are elusive for you, then replace them with apples or pears.

3½ pounds sweet potatoes (or yams)—peeled and diced

2½ cups persimmon puree—approx. 3 ripe persimmons (skin and seeds discarded, pureed in blender)

¼ cup thyme leaves—chopped

10 lemon verbena leaves—finely minced

1½ teaspoons curry powder

½ teaspoon cayenne pepper

1 teaspoon white pepper

1 tablespoon honey

1 orange—juiced

1 tablespoon salt

4 egg whites

Preheat the oven to 275°F.

Cook the sweet potatoes in boiling water until soft. While they are still warm, mash the potatoes into a smooth mass. Place the potatoes on a baking tray in the oven for 15 minutes to dry them out a bit.

In a large bowl, thoroughly combine the sweet potato, persimmon puree, thyme, verbena, curry powder, cayenne pepper, white pepper, honey, juiced orange, and salt together.

Beat the egg whites until stiff peaks are formed and gently fold them into the sweet potato mixture. Place in a 2-quart soufflé or casserole dish and bake for 40 minutes. Serve immediately.

Notes

There are two varieties of persimmons available to us, hachiya and fuyu. The former is tear-shape in appearance and contains a high concentration of tannins. If you eat underripe ones, you're left puckering for days. This variety should be used only when it is extremely soft and mushy. The fuyu is round and contains no tannins and may therefore be used firm.

CURRIED BRUSSELS SPROUTS

YIELDS 6 SERVINGS

I have enjoyed brussels sprouts since I was a little kid, when I would peel each leaf from the vegetable and slowly consume them. Finding brussels on the branch is so exciting to me. I'm never sure if I want to pick off the vegetable or land the stalk in a vase as a floral display, so I usually buy two. The stalk itself is edible (like broccoli stalks). You just have to peel away the fibrous outer layer to expose the more tender inner flesh. Cut the stalks into the same size as the sprouts and add them to the mix. Of course, if the ones on branch are not available, use ones that have already been plucked for you.

1 branch of brussels sprouts (about 2 inches in length with well-developed sprouts)—yields approximately 3 cups

1 cup chicken stock

1 cup water

4 ounces unsalted butter—at room temperature

2 tablespoons curry powder

Salt and freshly ground black pepper to taste

Remove the brussels sprouts from the branch, discard any damaged external leaves, and, using a paring knife, place a light "X" on the bottom end of each sprout. Place the sprouts in an 8-inch highsided pan, in a single layer, more or less. Add the stock and water, and bring to the boil over a high heat. Reduce the heat to a simmer and cook for 15 minutes.

Combine the butter and curry together to make an amalgamated mass. Then add this into the sprouts and season with salt and pepper. Cook an additional 10 minutes to reduce the remaining liquid to glaze the brussels sprouts. Serve hot.

SAUTÉED BURDOCK ROOT

This is a simple recipe that really highlights the sweet/earthiness of the burdock. It is possible to substitute salisfy for the burdock root. I do hope you become a fan of this much-undiscovered root vegetable.

- **1 pound burdock root**
- **1 tablespoon grapeseed oil**
- **2 tablespoons ver jus**
- **Salt and black pepper to taste**

Peel the burdock root and slice on angle about ¼ inch thick. Hold the pieces in a bowl of cold water to prevent them from turning brown.

Heat a 10-inch sauté pan over a high heat and add the grapeseed oil. Drain the burdock and add to the sauté pan while still wet. Any water still clinging to the burdock will splatter, so be careful when placing it in the hot pan. Cook until all the water has evaporated, about 5 minutes. Then add the ver jus and season with salt and pepper. Toss to incorporate, and serve immediately.

CELERY ROOT AND GREEN APPLE SALAD

YIELDS 6 TO 8 SERVINGS

The celery root is such a fragrant gift from the autumn harvest that it shows up in my stews, soups, sautés, and salads. You first have to get past the earth-encrusted bulb with its knobby exterior. I always suggest giving the celery root a quick wash before you start to peel it, just to avoid getting all that dirt on your work surface. Sometimes, if you are lucky, you will get the tops still attached to the bulb. They have great aromatic properties for a stock but unfortunately are way too fibrous to be used as a vegetable.

1 medium red onion

½ cup apple cider vinegar

2 pounds celery root

2 tart apples—such as Granny Smith, or Matsu

¼ cup chives—chopped

2 heaping tablespoons Dijon mustard

¼ cup extra virgin olive oil

Salt and freshly ground black pepper to taste

Slice the onion in half through its root base. By cutting the onion this way, you prevent it from falling apart on you, since all the leaves of the onion attach at the root end. Trim off the stem and peel away its outer layer. Slice the onion into a very thin julienne, which will actually be a half-moon shape. Toss the onions with the vinegar in a workbowl and let sit for 20 minutes.

In the meantime, peel the celery root by cutting off the root and stem portions to create a flat, stable surface. Using a paring or chef knife, peel the skin from the celery root. Given the thickness of the vegetable's skin, I find it much easier to use a knife than a vegetable peeler. Slice the celery root into ¼ inch panels and then cut those panels into ⅛-inch wide julienne strips. Add to the onions and vinegar and toss.

Core the apples and slice into ⅛-inch thick julienne strips and toss with the onion mixture along with the chives, mustard, olive oil, salt, and pepper.

This salad can be served warm or cold.

FENNEL SALAD

This delicious palate cleanser is a nod to an Italian dish that incorporates fennel, blood oranges, and walnuts. When blood oranges show up in December through February, add this crimson-fleshed fruit to the salad. You can keep this slad for up to 1 week in the refrigerator. You could add another dimension by using Black Mint Oil (page 115) in lieu of the almond oil.

> **2 fennel bulbs**
>
> **1 medium sweet Vidalia onion**
>
> **⅛ cup lemon verbena leaves—chopped**
>
> **⅛ cup Cherry Vinegar (page 113)**
>
> **¼ cup almond oil**
>
> **Salt and black pepper to taste**

Slice the fennel bulb and the onion into paper-thin slices. You may want to use a mandolin for this, or patiently use your best knife skills. Toss with the remaining ingredients and refrigerate overnight before serving.

DESSERTS

SPICED PEARS WRAPPED IN PHYLLO

YIELDS 6 SERVINGS

Phyllo seems to be a mystery to a lot of people, and yet it's really quite easy and versatile. Just be aware that phyllo dries out quickly, so whatever pieces you are not working with should be covered with a damp kitchen towel to prevent it from getting brittle. Similarly, part of the purpose of brushing the phyllo strips with the melted butter is to help keep them pliable. When buying phyllo, unless you get it freshly made, you will find it in the freezer selection of the grocery. I always reach to the back of the case to get the newest batch. It has about a 2-month freezer life. In this recipe you could easily do a variation with apples or just with dried fruits softened in warm water and some rum.

4 bosc pears—peeled and sliced ½-inch thick

½ cup dried cherries

2 tablespoons water

½ cup sugar

1 tablespoon cinnamon—ground

1 teaspoon nutmeg—ground

½ teaspoon allspice—ground

½ pound phyllo dough

1 pound unsalted butter—melted

1 cup cream

In a 2-quart saucepan, place the pears and dried cherries with water, and cook over a medium flame for 20 to 25 minutes. You want the pears to release their liquid and then let it evaporate. Cool the pears.

Mix ¼ cup of the sugar and all spices together and then toss with the pears.

Preheat the oven to 375°F.

Take two sheets of phyllo dough and cut into 1½-inch wide to 2-inch wide long strips. On a clean work surface lay down one strip and lightly brush it with the melted butter. Then place another strip down to make an "X" and brush lightly with melted butter. Then, using the remaining strips, fill in the "X," in a spoke-like pattern, brushing each strip with butter. Place about ½ cup of the pear mixture in the center of the phyllo. Then, starting with the last strip that was placed down, wrap it around the pears. Continue wrapping the pears, securing the phyllo strips snugly around the pear mixture. Brush the pear bundle lightly with melted butter and sprinkly the tops with sugar. Continue this pattern with the remaining phyllo and pear mixture. You will use about 12 strips of phyllo for each bundle.

Carefully place the pear bundles onto a baking tray and bake for 15 minutes, or until golden and crisp.

Slice and serve at room temperature garnished with whipped cream.

While the pears are baking, whip the cream using a handheld mixer.

QUINCE AND PEAR COMPOTE

YIELDS APPROXIMATELY 3 CUPS

The quince has a rather apple/pear flavor, but unlike its autumnal cousins, this fruit must be cooked to be palatable. Purchase fruit with a completely yellow skin, is dense to the touch, and heavy to feel. Its white flesh turns a brownish pink when cooked and will start to break down. This compote is so easy to put together and has a wonderful flavor, in a great part thanks to the ethereal quality of the quince. I have used it over shortcakes or even store-bought pound cake as a quick dessert. Or, try it in addition to traditional cranberry relish with a roast turkey.

2 quince (approximately 1 pound)

½ cup dried cherries

1 cup fresh orange juice

1 vanilla bean—split open

1 cup sugar

4 firm pears—peeled and cored

Peel and core the quince. Then cut the quince into 1-inch cubes.

In a 2-quart saucepan, place the quince, dried cherries, ½ cup of the orange juice, the vanilla bean, and sugar. Simmer over a medium-low flame for about 45 minutes. Cut the pears into 1-inch pieces and add to the quince mixture along with the remaining orange juice. Simmer another 30 minutes. Cool completely in the refrigerator before serving.

APPLE CRISP TOWERS

YIELDS 6 SERVINGS

These are really impressive and easy to pull off. Vertical food is always a showstopper. I like to sandwich ice cream between the apple and phyllo pieces as the mortar to hold it together. However, you could use a curd, whipped cream, or, for a lower-fat version, yogurt.

2 cups sugar

1 tablespoon cinnamon—ground

1 teaspoon allspice—ground

½ teaspoon nutmeg—ground

5 medium-size apples (such as Cortland, Jonagold, or Empire)

1 pound phyllo dough

½ pound unsalted butter—melted

Parchment paper

1 pint vanilla ice-cream

Preheat the oven to 350°F.

Mix the sugar, cinnamon, nutmeg, and allspice together.

Peel the apples and remove their seed centers using an apple corer. Cut the apples into rings—getting 5 rings from each apple. Toss the rings with the spice mixture to coat well, reserving a bit of the spices.

Lay the phyllo out on a clean work surface and cover with a damp kitchen towel (when phyllo dries out, it gets very brittle and cannot be successfully worked with). Take a sheet of phyllo, and lay it out separately. Brush with some butter, starting at the edges, since they tend to dry out first. Then lay another sheet on top of the buttered one, and still a third—brushing each additional sheet with butter. Cut out disks that are just slightly larger than the apple rings, approximately 3 inches in diameter. Use a cookie cutter or a wide enough glass as your template. The phyllo disks will be 3 sheets thick.

On a baking sheet, place one disk with an apple ring on top, then cover with a second phyllo disk. Sprinkle with the leftover spiced sugar, and drizzle with a little butter. Lay out the phyllo in this manner until you've used them all.

Cover the phyllo-apple disks with a piece of parchment paper and place another baking tray right on top of it to lightly weight down the phyllo-apple disks. This will help prevent the phyllo from curling while being baked. Place in the oven and bake until golden and crisp, about 5 to 10 minutes. Remove from the baking sheet while still warm or the caramelized sugar will stick. Place the phyllo-apple disks on a cooling rack and cool completely.

Assemble by sandwiching two to three layers of the phyllo-apples together with ice cream between each layer.

ORANGE/LEMON CURD

Whenever I make angel food cake I always end up with a slew of yolks. This is a great way to use them. For Valentine's Day I'll make an angel food cake and then use blood orange juice instead of the orange and lemon juices here. The color is intense. This curd has about a 1-week shelf life in the refrigerator.

> 2 oranges—juiced (about ¾ cup)
>
> 1 lemon—juiced (about ¼ cup)
>
> 8 large egg yolks
>
> ½ cup sugar
>
> ¼ pound unsalted butter—cut into small pieces

In a 6-cup bowl (either glass or stainless steel) place the orange juice, lemon juice, yolks, and sugar, and mix to combine thoroughly. Sit the bowl over a double boiler of steaming water and whisk until the mixture thickens, about 10 to 15 minutes. Make sure that the workbowl does not touch the water in the bottom of the pan or sit too high up on the rim of the pan. These two positions are the hottest spots and can cause the yolks to curdle. Be careful not to scramble the egg yolks in the mixture, and if the water gets too hot, lower the heat or shut off completely. Keep the egg mixture moving until thickened to the point where it coats the back of a spoon. Remove from the heat and whisk in the butter pieces to thoroughly incorporate. Chill the curd completely in the refrigerator with a piece of plastic wrap sitting right on the curd to prevent a skin from forming.

Serve well-chilled over fresh fruits and a slice of pound cake. Or use it instead of ice cream in the Apple Crisp Towers (page 172).

MAPLE SYRUP AND DRIED FRUIT COMPOTE

YIELDS APPROXIMATELY 3 CUPS

By the deep of winter I am so weary of apples, pears, sweet potatoes, and the lot. However, the fruits flown in from other parts of the world don't thrill me either. So inevitably I started using dried fruits. You can dry your own fruits by placing them in a dehydrator or in a 175°F oven for 5 to 12 hours (depending on their size and density). To keep my dried fruit from developing mold, I store them in the freezer.

- **1 cup fresh orange juice**
- **¼ cup golden raisins**
- **¼ cup dried apricots—chopped**
- **¼ cup dried cranberries**
- **¼ cup dried apples—chopped**
- **1½ cups maple syrup**

In a 4-quart saucepan, heat the orange juice to a boil over medium heat, and then add the dried fruit. Lower to a simmer and cook for 10 minutes to plump the fruit. Add the maple syrup, and cook for 5 minutes longer.

Serve warm over shortcakes and whipped cream, or over morning pancakes or plain yogurt.

BEVERAGES

APPLE SHOCHU
YIELDS 2 QUARTS

Shochu is a distilled spirit from Japan made from rice, potato, or barley. It's referred to at times as a Downtown Napoleon (brandy). I am most fond of the rice-distilled variety, which, along with the others, can be found in better liquor stores and Japanese markets. While living in Japan I was quite in the habit of having a Lemon Sour, which is shochu and lemonade over ice. Here I have taken the *Ringo Sour,* which is apple juice and shochu over ice, and infused it right into the bottle. Serve this shochu over ice mixed with apple cider. Make a festive holiday martini using the Apple Shochu and a splash of hard cider garnished with a cinnamon stick straight up.

750 milliliter bottle shochu

3 tart apples (such as Pepin, Granny Smith, or Matsu)

Wash and quarter the apples, or smaller, so they fit through the mouth of a 4-quart jar. Add the shochu and cover with a tight-fitting lid. Store in a cool, dark spot for 1 month.

Pour through a funnel lined with a few layers of cheesecloth. After the liquid has been strained through, push down on the fruit to extract out some additional flavor. Store at room temperataure with a tight-fitting lid for 1 year. Serve this over ice in a tall glass with a sliced apple garnish.

SPICED ALMOND LIQUEUR

YIELDS 4 LITERS

Like so many recipes, this came to me in a dream, though I will add I was not inebriated as I lay my head down. Instead, I was thinking of an Italian beverage made from walnuts that sits through the summer months waiting for autumn's uncorking. It took a year and half before I was able to fulfill my nocturnal vision, since I could not find green almonds. Finally, on a jaunt to an Indian neighborhood in Queens, New York, I stumbled upon the almonds in a wonderful green market and proceeded to set up my vision. It was worth the wait. If fresh greens almonds are elusive to you, you may want to try this with whole unblanched almonds. I was too stubborn.

1 teaspoon whole clove

1 tablespoon mace blades

2 whole nutmeg

6 cinnamon sticks (about each 3 inches in length)

3 whole vanilla beans

2 pounds whole green almonds—washed well of any dirt

1.75 liters pure grain alcohol

2¾ cup Simple Syrup (see margin note)

5 cups bottled water

½ cup honey

In a 2-gallon glass jar with a tight-fitting lid, place the cloves, mace blades, nutmeg, cinnamon sticks, vanilla beans, and whole almonds. Pour the pure grain alcohol over the spices and cover securely. Place in a dark, cool spot and let cure for 2 months.

After the 2 months, strain the alcohol mixture through several layers of cheesecloth, and discard the spices and almonds. Stir the Simple Syrup, water, and honey into the alcohol. I tend to warm the honey in some of the water to more easily distribute it throughout. Let this sit for 1 more week with a tight-fitting lid. The liquid will cloud up and eventually

Notes

Simple Syrup is a solution of water and sugar that is cooked over a medium-low flame till clear and then boiled for a few minutes. For this recipe I use 7 cups water and 4 cups sugar to make the syrup. This syrup will last 1 month stored at room temperature in a jar with a tight-fitting lid.

that cloudiness should rise to the top. After 1 week, strain the entire mixture through a double thickness of paper coffee filters. The size of your coffee filter cone will determine how many times you will have to change the paper filters. I usually change them at least 4 times.

CLEMENTINE CELLO

YIELDS APPROXIMATELY 2 GALLONS

This potent beverage has the look of Orange Crush, but be warned it is strictly an adult drink. It's a variation on Lemon Cello, a southern Italy liqueur that I learned to make when visiting Positano on the Amalfi coast. The town of Sorrento, just north of Positano, in the shadow of Mount Vesuvius, sits on volcanic earth that produces the most luscious lemons on earth. Having been so spoiled by those tart beauties I have replaced them with clementines. If you find Meyer lemons or key limes in your area, you just may want to try yet another version.

16 clementine oranges

1.5 liters pure grain alcohol

1.5 liters water

4½ cups sugar

Place the clementines in a pot of boiling water and blanch them for 30 to 60 seconds. Remove them to a colander and run under cold tap water. I take this step to rid the clementines of any paraffin wax that may have been added. This food-grade wax helps to extend the fruit's shelf life, but in this application it would just end up in the finished product.

Peel the skins from the clementines and then carefully remove the excess white pith. I use a paring knife and just scrape off the pith. Place the cleaned zest in a three-gallon glass jar that has a tight-fitting lid. Add the pure grain alcohol and cover. Let the mixture sit for 7 days in a cool place out of direct sunlight.

Bring the water and sugar to a boil in a 4-quart pot and lower the temperature to a simmer and cook the mixture for 5 minutes. Cool the sugar solution completely.

After 7 days, strain the alcohol mixture into the sugar solution (after it is absolutely cooled) through a few layers of cheesecloth or a clean coffee filter. Gently press down on the zest to extract any additional flavor into the sugar/alcohol solution. Discard the zest. Let the mixture sit 1 more week in a sealed glass jar. Then strain the mixture again through a few layers of cheesecloth into bottles and store in the freezer. This is best served ice-cold in a shot glass and sipped.

VINEGARS AND OILS

GRAPE VINEGAR
YIELDS APPROXIMATELY 2 QUARTS

Whenever I taste this vinegar, the grape jelly that I loved so much as a kid comes right to mind. Using concord grapes adds to this experience as they produce a wonderful fragrance and a color that is deep, dark purple. Each grape variety is going to offer its own special flavor. If you use a white grape, I would consider using a white wine or champagne vinegar instead of the apple cider vinegar because of its milder flavor and lack of color. I have used this vinegar in a vinaigrette for a duck salad or just simply over some of my favorite greens.

1 pound grapes such as Concord, Muscat, Sauvignon Cabernet

1½ quarts raw apple cider vinegar

Wash the grapes and remove them from their stems.

Place the grapes in a 4-quart glass jar and crush them down. Add the vinegar and cover with a tight-fitting lid. Place in a cool, dark place for 2 weeks.

Strain the vinegar mixture through a sieve lined with a cheesecloth or a clean coffee filter. Store in a glass jar with a tight-fitting lid for up to 6 months.

SPICY CABBAGE

YIELDS 16 SERVINGS

I don't know what is with me and pickles, but I love them. This recipe reminds me of a trip to Korea and all the *kimchee* eaten there, though unlike that ubiquitous Korean accompaniment, this pickled cabbage is not nearly as pungent. The small Asian-style chilies do give this recipe a kick. You could expand the pickle by adding carrots, diakons (mild Asian radishes), and cucumbers.

> 1 head white cabbage or Napa cabbage (approx. 2 pounds)
>
> 2 to 3 red bird's eye chilies—seeded and diced
>
> 3-inch long piece of ginger root—peeled and julienned
>
> 1 tablespoon turmeric—ground
>
> ½ cup cilantro leaves—chopped
>
> 4 garlic cloves—chopped
>
> 2 teaspoons Thai fish Sauce
>
> 1 cup rice vinegar
>
> ⅛ cup soy sauce

Cut the cabbage into ⅛'s and remove the core. Place in a 1-gallon glass or ceramic container with a nonmetallic lid. If you use a plastic container, you will never get the smell of this pickle out of it, so be prepared to dedicate that container to this recipe.

Bring all the other ingredients to a boil in a 4-cup saucepan over medium heat, and simmer for 10 minutes. Pour this hot mix over the cabbage. Cover and store in the refrigerator for 3 days to 1 week before you start to enjoy. It will last about 1 to 2 months.

NOTES

NOTES

NOTES

With love, I offer
my being's exuding skill . . .
Call them to dinner

BIBLIOGRAPHY

Rosalind Creasy, *The Gardener's Handbook of Edible Plants*. San Francisco: Sierra Club Books, 1986.

Serge D'Amico and Francois Fortin, eds., *The Visual Food Encyclopedia*. New York: Simon and Schuster Macmillan Company, 1996.

Dave Dewitt, *The Chile Pepper Encyclopedia*. New York: William Morrow and Company, 1999.

Bert Greene, *The Grains Cookbook*. New York: Workman Publishing, 1988.

Sharon Tyler Herbst, *Food Lover's Companion*. Hauppauge, NY: Baron's Educational Series, Inc., 1995.

Elisabeth Lambert Ortiz, *The Encyclopedia of Herbs, Spices and Flavorings*. New York: DK Publishing, Inc., 1992.

Helena Radecka, *The Fruit and Nut Book*. New York: McGraw-Hill, 1984.

Jeanne Rose, *Jeanne Rose: Herbal Body Book: The Herbal Way to Natural Beauty & Health for Men & Women*. New York: Perigee Books, 1976.

Elizabeth Schneider, *Uncommon Fruits and Vegetables*. New York: William Morrow and Company, 1998 (re-issue).

J.G. Vaughan and C.A. Geissler, *The New Oxford Book of Food Plants*. New York: Oxford University Press, 1997.

Jane Walker, *Creative Cooking with Spices*. London: Apple Press, 1985.